# Speaking Up

## A Book for Every Woman Who Talks

by Janet Stone and Jane Bachner

Illustrations by Catherine Tvirbutas

Carroll & Graf Publishers/Richard Gallen
New York

First Carroll & Graf Publishers/Richard Gallen edition, 1994

Carroll & Graf Publishers, Inc.
260 Fifth Avenue
New York, NY 10001

Manufactured in the United States of America

# ACKNOWLEDGMENTS

Janet would like to thank her Wednesday Night Team, The Whine Line, Kai Hennig and Maureen Farrell of Waveform Women's Video, Jen Wakefield, Linda Nunes and Dialing for Dollars (Jayne Nelson, Mary Fillmore, Suzanne Grill, Judith Musick, Ventana Weir and Nicki Kersey). Special thanks to workshop participants from coast to coast whose principled outspokenness provides ongoing inspiration.

Jane would like to thank Frank Bachner who rarely falters, Linda McJannet, Pat Kosinar, Toby Conrad, Susan Heyman, Marie Hermann, Marcy Balter, Gwen Nagel, Jane Coutts, Marge and Tom Donnell and especially Will, Tom and Kate Bachner for their love and support.

We both appreciate the fine efforts of Joanne Dolinar, Peter Skutches, Ann Krueger Spivack and Catherine Tvirbutas.

Unlearning to not speak

Blizzards of paper
in slow motion sift through her.
In nightmares she suddenly recalls
a class she signed up for
but forgot to attend.
Now it is too late.
Now it is time for finals: losers will be shot.
Phrases of men who lectured her
drift and rustle in piles:
Why don't you speak up?
Why are you shouting?
You have the wrong answer,
wrong line, wrong face.
They tell her she is womb-man,
babymachine, mirror image, toy,
earth mother and penis-poor,
a dish of synthetic strawberry ice cream
rapidly melting.
She grunts to a halt.
She must learn again to speak
starting with I
starting with We
starting as the infant does
with her own true hunger
and pleasure
and rage.

Marge Piercy
From *To Be of Use*

# CONTENTS

**INTRODUCTION/** The reason for this book        xiii

CHAPTER ONE/ **OUT FROM BEHIND THE CURTAIN**  1
Women's gradual emergence into public life as speakers.
How we think about ourselves, present ourselves and how
others perceive us. The barriers, within and without, to successful communication.

CHAPTER TWO/ **EVALUATING AND
STRENGTHENING YOUR SPEECH PERSONALITY**  9
Common means of self-defeat. How nervousness shows:
self-trivializing language, inappropriate smiling, "invisible
woman" body language, high pitch and whisper talk.
Strengthening your conversational habits; eliminating unconscious apology.

CHAPTER THREE/ **NERVES**        32
Useful strategies for managing your fears. Recovering

from mistakes. From stage fright to "preparation energy." Solving the problem: prevention, preparation, recovery and practice.

### CHAPTER FOUR/ HOW TO ARRANGE A SUCCESSFUL SPEECH                                      56
Eliminating unpleasant surprises. How to use your liaison—the secret of the pros.

### CHAPTER FIVE/ WRITING TO BE HEARD                                      71
The differences between writing a talk and writing anything else. The elements of persuasive speaking.

### CHAPTER SIX/ YOUR PROPS: NOTES AND VISUAL AIDS                                      97
The practical and psychological advantages of managing your tools.

### CHAPTER SEVEN/ REHEARSAL AND PRESENTATION                                      113
How to do the best you can with what you've got. Impression management, faking confidence. Relying on thorough preparation.

### CHAPTER EIGHT/ QUESTIONS AND ANSWERS                                      134
Handling hostile audiences, staying in charge. Advice on tricky, boring or irrelevant questions and managing those who ask them.

### CHAPTER NINE/ AN INTRODUCTION IS A SPEECH                                      152
"Oral resumes"; how to describe yourself, how to prepare an audience for a speaker. Establishing your image.

CHAPTER TEN/ **SPEAKING IMPROMPTU**          166
How to be articulate without preparation. Thinking on
your feet.

CHAPTER ELEVEN/ **TALKING IN GROUPS**          176
How to avoid being interrupted, having your ideas stolen
and being intimidated at meetings. How to organize and
lead a meeting.

CHAPTER TWELVE/ **MEDIA**          193
Getting results from telephone calls, radio and television
interviews and the press.

CHAPTER THIRTEEN/ **FINAL THOUGHTS**          209

NOTES          212

BIBLIOGRAPHY          214

ABOUT THE AUTHORS          216

# INTRODUCTION

We each talk, with more or less success, all day. How seriously we are taken, how often our point of view prevails, how well people get to know us, how far we advance in our work and how successful we are in our personal relationships often depend upon our ability to express ourselves clearly and with ease and assurance.

The information in *Speaking Up* focuses on examples from meetings, formal presentations and workshops, but it must be clear that every time you open your mouth you are making a speech. Except for muttering to yourself in the bathroom, all speaking is public speaking. When you argue with a delivery person, give instructions to babysitters, fire an employee, explain your feelings to a friend, answer questions in an interview or talk on the phone you are using your communications skills. If you aren't forceful and confident in those situations, a larger forum will only exaggerate your weaknesses. The attitudes, diction, mannerisms, body language and voice that you use in private go with you into more public settings.

Unfortunately, women have been taught to form habits of word use, inflection, style—and, indeed, silence—that directly contradict the purpose of communication: exchanging ideas and sharing feelings. This book will touch on habits of speech that get in our way, undermine our confidence, reflect and perpetuate our second-class status and prevent us from getting what we need.

The basic approach to more effective talking is to shape up everyday speech habits. You can't use "y'know," "um . . . uh," gesture wildly or whisper your way through life and expect somehow to speak differently when at a podium.

We hope *Speaking Up* will accomplish three things:

- Show you how to camouflage and eventually cure nervousness;

- Dispel the mystique surrounding "speechmaking" to show it for exactly what it is—talking;

- Help you become more confident and articulate all the time, not just for special occasions or audiences.

It is both especially important and especially difficult for women to learn to speak well in public. Both authors experienced the panic, the damp palms and the nausea, and we *know* overcoming the fear is hard. Speaking is such a personal activity; one's personality and physical appearance are very much involved and on view. The stereotypes and myths about women that have affected us over the years have affected audiences, too, and stereotypes often determine how we are perceived and how our messages are received.

If speaking up is so difficult, why bother learning how to do it? First, self-assertion is an important part of almost everything we want to do. Obviously politics, teaching, management, volunteer work, sales, the law and many other career/work choices demand poised self-expression. Second, being able to talk well makes life more fun. Finally, speaking out is a fundamental right of free people, one that was forbidden to women for many years and one that we must not, we will not, lose again.

Until the first edition of *Speaking Up* was published, we could not find a book we could recommend enthusiastically to our students. Older texts still made the assumption that women rarely addressed groups. They used abundant "men only" examples. This new edition of *Speaking Up* is more practical than textbooks that don't mention hot flashes, and more accessible than private coaching (which can cost as much as $6,000 per day). Whether you are a novice who hopes to become adequate, or a good speaker who hopes to become excellent, this book is written for you.

Every woman is unique and valuable; your ideas, your experience and your understanding are important. We hope to help you polish and share that experience, because we believe it will do all of us good to hear you.

# CHAPTER ONE

---

# Out From Behind the Curtain

The World Anti-Slavery Convention held in London in 1840 was a turning point for American women. Some of the abolitionist groups that represented the United States were made up entirely of women and, of course, their delegates to the convention were women. The male delegates objected strenuously to the women's participation, and after great debate voted to seat only men. Women were forced to sit behind a curtain to hear the proceedings. They could not speak; they had no vote. These women had worked long and hard for the anti-slavery cause which they so deeply believed in. They had a great deal to say; to be denied a chance to say it was a bitter experience. Two of the women behind the curtain became good friends and allies that summer: Lucretia Mott, a Quaker who had long been active in reform movements, and Elizabeth Cady Stanton, a much younger woman who was in London on her honeymoon. They talked about the irony of their situation, they talked about the inequalities from which they suffered, and talked about what they could do about it. On one occasion, Elizabeth Cady Stanton went to hear her new friend give a speech in a local meeting house. She had never heard a woman speak in public (few people had) and Mrs. Stanton was thrilled.

In the nineteenth century the right to freedom of speech was not customarily extended to women. Although it did not offend Victorian sensibilities for women to work quietly for good causes (behind a curtain), it was considered outrageous for a woman to speak in public ... unwomanly, unladylike and unnatural. However, Lucretia Mott, like many of the early leaders of the women's rights movement, was a Quaker. The Society of Friends encouraged women to speak in meeting and even allowed them to be ordained. Mrs. Mott had been ordained a minister at the age of twenty-eight and had spoken often.

Elizabeth Cady Stanton was impressed. Gradually she became aware of the overwhelming difficulty facing her and the other women working in the abolitionist cause; in order to be effective in freeing the slaves, women first would have to free themselves from the restraints and strictures of Victorian femininity.

Eight years later at the first women's rights convention in Seneca Falls, New York, Mrs. Stanton made her own "maiden" speech, summing up what has moved a great many women since to begin speaking up:

> I should feel exceedingly diffident to appear before you at this time, having never before spoken in public, were I not nerved by a sense of right and duty....

Women have changed laws and customs since Mrs. Stanton's 1848 speech. We now speak in public every day on a great variety of issues, for many causes and often just for fun. In fact, women in the Senate, the House of Representatives, in state legislatures, women governors and college presidents could be called professional speakers. Certainly the thousands of women broadcasters who appear on radio and television every day speak for a living.

We have discredited those Victorian rules of womanly behavior that kept our foremothers quiet and frustrated in 1840, but underlying taboos linger. As lawyers, fundraisers and community activists, we are still uncomfortable (without understanding why) taking a stand, arguing a point or leading a group. We may avoid a promotion because the new job would demand much more public speaking. We may not confront the city council because we would feel uneasy standing up and challenging the speaker. Worst of all, we may just quietly go along in some situations because it feels risky to make noise about it or because we convince ourselves that "it was only a minor point, anyway."

But unless we can speak up, persuade and convince, unless we have the power of speech, unless we have a say in what goes on, we are not in control of our lives. What are these ideas about "femininity" we have inherited that make it difficult for us to speak effectively?

The most important assets of a good speaker are a strong voice, good eye contact, erect posture, clarity, decisiveness and self-confidence. Are these assets "feminine"? Not in the traditional view. In fact, "femininity" is associated with silence.

"Her voice was ever soft, gentle and low; an excellent thing in woman." Many women grew up with that quotation; it served as a standard. Yet in the passage of *King Lear* in which that line is spoken, Lear's daughter Cordelia is dead and Lear in his grief is saying that she may not really be dead, it was always hard to hear her. As Dorothy Parker said when they told her Calvin Coolidge was dead: "How can they tell?"

Many of us were reared by parents who held conventional ideas of feminine decorum: women do not bellow, they do not shout, they do not declaim or orate, they should not even speak much above a whisper. A chilling example of this self-defeating conduct is the difficulty some women experience in self-defense classes trying to overcome their socialization enough to shout and holler when being attacked. Women who have great clear loud voices are still made to feel ashamed. How often a lover or husband will say, "Don't you scream at me!" the moment a woman raises her voice even slightly. When someone is opposed to a woman's point of view, he or she almost invariably mentions that her style is "shrill."

"Harridan," "termagant," "scold," "fishwife," "shrew," "nag," "magpie," "virago" . . . the list of insults for women who speak up is long. It is interesting to note that many of these words also mean ugly, sexually foul or old. There is no parallel male character anywhere in tradition; that is, there is no word for a man whose voice annoys people. (The obvious exception is the stereotype of the male homosexual—and his behavior is clearly labeled "feminine.") Women are so fearful of seeming abrasive that we mumble and mutter, and no one can hear a word we say. A good strong loud voice carries conviction and authority, and that is exactly why girls and women are discouraged from having one.

Before you say "not me," or "not any more" take a good look at yourself on videotape. You may be in for a surprise.

A good speaker establishes eye contact with her audience. She uses that eye contact to get feedback and to establish herself as open and straightforward. People in some cultures interpret looking down as a sign of respect; however, white Anglo Saxons usually perceive shifty eyes as dishonest and a direct gaze as sincere. Women are expected to disregard this rule. We aren't encouraged to look people directly in the eye; instead we are told to avert our eyes, not to stare; we are taught how to drop our gaze seductively. A woman who looks someone directly in the eye runs the risk of being thought aggressive or pushy. Worse, an open direct gaze from a woman can be misconstrued as a sexual invitation. According to this double standard, a "bold" look is not simply a courageous one. What is considered positive, admirable conduct in a man and in people in general is viewed as wrong and unnatural in a woman. Different words can describe the same behavior with the negative terms applying primarily to women. For example, "wit" in men is "cattiness" in women. To make matters worse, the standards by which people are believed, accepted, promoted and elected are the standards for men and for "people." A woman behaving as she was taught to behave—that is, acting "feminine,"—disqualifies herself as an authority and is rarely taken seriously.

A Pastoral Letter from the Council of Congregationalist Ministers of Massachusetts attacked the idea of women speaking in public when they first began to do so early in the 1800s. It summed up rather nicely an opinion still around today:

> If the vine, whose strength and beauty is to lean on the trellis-work and half conceal its cluster, thinks to assume the independence and the overshadowing nature of the elm, it will not only cease to bear fruit, but fall in shame and dishonor into the dust.

Don't underestimate how growing up without a view of women in public situations inhibits our ability to speak. We watch women in public life, even today, struggle to project authority and power without losing their "warmth," and we are often critical when they fail, when they sound either too tough or too weak. What's worse, rather than inspiring us, watching their struggle often makes us afraid to try because to do so is to defy the traditional image of women.

Women are supposed to be beautiful—that's axiomatic. We get plenty of approval if we are gorgeous, young and well dressed. Unfortunately, the percentage of women who are beautiful (according to the conventions of the day) is about the same as the percentage of men who are beautiful—very small. Most of us have come to terms with not being "beautiful" and get along fairly well most of the time. We only become obsessed with how we look on rare occasions.

Standing in front of a group of strangers who are all looking you over is definitely one of those occasions. Making a speech can trigger every last one of your insecurities; it takes willpower not to hunch over and hide. Strong self-confident posture is absolutely vital to any speaker, but very hard to achieve when we know that our skin "should" be clearer, our teeth whiter, our hair shinier, our breasts bigger or smaller, our muscles firmer and our clothes completely different.

Although women today deplore the relentless conditioning to be obsessed with physical appearance, we can't change the brainwashing of a lifetime overnight, or shut off the advertising spigot. It is no wonder the nasty lurking fear that we will be thought unattractive is so powerful.

It doesn't help much to move from physical appearance to the broader area of "charm." Here, too, we must struggle against daily reinforcement of traditional ideas of what is "charming" in a woman. Unfortunately, in many cases charm is equated with a vague, indecisive lighthearted gaiety, or with being a wonderful "listener." A good speaker needs to be as precise and concrete as possible; the last thing any audience wants is rambling, giggly nonsense. A good public speech may be warm, but it first must be strong, assertive and direct. Although a speaker does respond to her audience, she is never a "listener." She's doing the talking.

A woman's need for approval is not evidence of wobbly self-esteem or a weak personality. When a woman blames herself for her fear she is ignoring real rewards and real punishments. Without the approval of the powerful, a woman may lose a scholarship, a job or the custody of her children.

Anyone who takes on the responsibility of speaking her mind will encounter resistance. It is natural for people to argue, to resist being convinced, to insist that the speaker "prove it." That's what makes interesting question-and-answer periods and good conversation at dinner. However, women often encounter a specific resistance that is both annoying and disruptive. Many meet any woman's words with a skepticism based on a subconscious conviction that women don't know what they are talking about. We encounter more than our fair share of grave doubts, open amusement, boredom and even hostility. In fact, a woman may be ignored even when she is the sole authority. (Perhaps you know the story about the woman in labor who says to her obstetrician, "I am in great pain," and he says, "No, you're not.'') After you have spoken well, documented your evidence and proved your point, the brass may be momentarily impressed, but the next day you will have to begin proving your competence and earning your credibility all over again . . . and again . . . and again.

Audience hostility may be caused by a genuine disagreement with your stand on the issues or it may be that your personality irritates someone. Unfortunately, the "problem" also might be your race, age, religion or national origin. Audience hostility may take the form of open vocal aggression (teasing, heckling, catcalling, boos, nasty personal questions) or be a more silent variety such as crossed arms or yawns. Either way, speaking to a hostile group of people is unpleasant, especially if you are already fighting an internal censor who is saying, "You shouldn't have opened your mouth." It may be particularly upsetting to women. Pleasing men once was an economic necessity for many women; marriage was often the only available job. Our skill, knowledge or ability was not sufficient; we also had to gain social approval. But it isn't merely Jurassic Age brainwashing that silences us or a legacy of subordination to men that eats away at our self-assurance. Women fear the everyday punishment for "getting out of line" usually meted out through subtle professional exclusion, isolation and insufficient support.

This fear hampers a woman's ability to speak well. A good speaker cannot be afraid of disagreement, criticism or even anger. She must not have a chip on her shoulder and must be able to maintain good humor.

We want *Speaking Up* to help you develop the determination to say what you think anytime, anywhere, with self-confidence or without it. You must be the final judge of your performance. As Maya Angelou says: "If a woman allows other people's definitions of her achievements to encroach on her own understanding of her achievements, it will wipe her out."

There remain challenges (and advantages) unique to women speakers. This does not mean that women have difficulties and do it wrong while men have no problems and do it right. Many men suffer torments when required to speak in public—even though listeners of both sexes may unconsciously over-value men's ideas and contributions.

Not only does a female speaker have to deal with stage fright, hostility and her own fear of failure, she also has to learn to deal with the complexities of success. Public speaking can be very powerful. A good speech can persuade, arouse, inflame and change the course of events.

Because women are new to this kind of power, we don't take it for granted. We don't think it is our automatic right. We have fought long and hard to gain entry into the decision-making circles and we want to be correct, to do the right thing. This sense of responsibility for the consequences of our words and our decisions coexists with (and can be complicated by) our desire for fuller acceptance as team members in the organizations where we work. At times, our views, our words and our leadership are on a collision course with those who seem very sure of themselves and have power over our careers.

Speaking your mind is an integral part of participation in life. "Femininity," like any other bad habit, can be unlearned. Self-defeating behavior patterns that make someone less effective as a speaker inhibit her in all other facets of her life as well. Those habits can be changed. It isn't simple, but it isn't impossible either; it does take practice. Almost all of us are born speakers; we had to be taught to sit down and shut up. Now is the time to unlearn that teaching.

# CHAPTER TWO

# Evaluating and Strengthening Your Speech Personality

> *"It's not what you say, it's how you say it."*
> —American cliché

A good speaker is like a good athlete: she makes it look easy. She has taken a hard look at herself and developed her skills in each of the categories that are fundamental to good speech: body language, word choice, voice quality, emotional tone and personal interaction with the audience. She is aware of the ways in which women have been encouraged to undermine their strengths and defeat their purposes, and she struggles to overcome that programming.

But it *looks* easy; the audience is aware only of a smooth relaxed presentation. If you have been in that audience and thought, "Sure, it's easy for her but I couldn't do it," we're going to try to change your mind. We think you can do it and in this chapter tell how to identify traits to eliminate and good habits to incorporate in your speaking.

A woman who thinks talking in small groups isn't a problem, and claims she only gets stuck when speaking to a big audience, usually isn't as fluent as she would like to believe in normal conversation. Our techniques for improvement involve better daily habits, not magical schemes for pulling oneself together at the last minute for a big speech.

Frightened people have a way of talking that is as easy to identify as a Brooklyn accent. Many women announce that they are both full of doubt and eager to please every time they open their mouths. Even when that self-doubt is exactly the reverse of what we want to communicate, it comes out in habits of speech so engrained that we don't even notice them. It is ironic that speech, which can be our most potent ally in the struggle for change, can so easily defeat us.

There are hundreds of self-defeating speech habits. This chapter will touch on some of the major ones, to which your initial response may be, "I don't do *that*." Perhaps you don't. But just so you will be sure, we'll start by describing how you can find out exactly what you do: how you talk and how you sound.

There is only one perfect tool for analyzing your speaking habits: videotape. A film of you in action allows you to watch and listen as if you were your own audience. We videotape participants in our classes because video reveals all that a tape recorder keeps hidden: facial tics and grimaces, poor posture, spasmodic gestures and so forth.

Two other good ways of evaluating your speech habits are listening to tape recordings and watching yourself rehearse in a full-length mirror. Most of us are surprised (and disappointed) the first time we hear our voice on tape. The common response is "Oh, no—that can't be me." You may hear fillers (um, er, uh), a nasal quality, high pitch, giggling, false starts or any number of other horrors. But hearing yourself as others hear you is an important first step to a great improvement. Listen to yourself—others do.

Record yourself having a telephone conversation with a friend or record a family dinner hour. Make recordings of yourself reading, reciting speeches or telling jokes. Tape yourself having a fight with someone you love. Try to get a realistic sample of how you sound in as many situations as possible.

When you have a lot on tape sit down and listen to it care-

fully. Ask a few colleagues or friends what they like about the
way you talk and what they would suggest you do differently.
You may get an earful. "Well, aside from your mumbling ...,"
"It's the flapping arms that really drive me crazy. ...." Compare their observations with your own and select one or two
specific things about your speaking that you wish to change.

Now, what are you going to listen and look for?


## Watching Body Language

Body language is the eloquent message we send with our stance
and gestures. When what we say with our body contradicts our
words, people believe the gestures and expressions. Most body
language interpretation is common sense. Slouch and you look
tired and discouraged. Hang your head and refuse to face people
and you appear embarrassed or ashamed. Clench your teeth or
your fists and you communicate anger or fear. A list of the
peculiar gestures people make out of sheer nervousness would
be endless. Some common distracting movements are foot tapping, finger drumming, lip biting, cuticle picking, nose wrin-
kling, head scratching and ring twisting. You appear less than
sure of yourself brushing or tossing your hair out of your face,
pushing your glasses up, pulling your clothes around and playing with something (a pencil, book, notes or whatever you've
been able to carry to the podium).

Some women have adopted a completely self-effacing "invisible woman" body language. Their message seems to be
"Don't take me seriously, I don't take myself seriously. In fact,
I am not even here." Those of us who are afflicted sit down
in a way that won't offend the chair, continually walk around
the wastebasket rather than move it and have been known to
say "Excuse me" when we walk into a wall. Rather than incon-
venience the microphone by pulling it to mouth level, we end
up looking like contortionists. Although it's a rare speaker who

can sneak to the front of the room without awakening the audience, we have been known to try.

We say "I'm sorry" in body language by talking with our hands clasped in front of us or talking with our arms behind our backs.

Every day our culture encourages us to be self-conscious about our bodies and ashamed of our many figure flaws. We are quite rightly uneasy about being objectified sexually. Those women who have large breasts often won't stand up straight for fear of seeming brazen. In fact, most women have adopted one form or another of "ladylike" behavior. When we are self-effacing or ineffectual in the way we occupy space it is often because we are shriveling in anxious response to a negative cue from someone who finds strong, direct communication threatening.

The remedy for all this is exactly what your mother told you. Stand up straight, look people in the eye and quit fidgeting. Force yourself to let your arms hang loosely at your sides, force yourself to hold your head up (not cocked to the side) and talk. It takes supreme self-discipline to just stand there. It follows that if you can manage to just stand there, the audience will believe you are confident. You may even feel confident.

## Making Eye Contact

The simple act of looking someone squarely in the eye is more persuasive than a hundred words. Eye contact in a presentation does not mean quickly scanning the audience and returning to your notes. Look at one person and hold her gaze until there is some response. Then turn to someone on the other side of the room and hold her gaze; then focus on someone in the back. Eye contact is power. By looking someone directly in the eye you make real contact, and invite a response.

Pretending not to see or hear things has been a traditional ''ladylike'' way of dealing with unpleasantness. Some of us try to pretend the audience isn't there by staring over their heads or up at the ceiling or down at our notes. At best this causes the audience to lose interest, and it can alienate some audience members.

## Inappropriate Smiling, Joking and Laughing

Girls are softened up in school, worn down, and prepared psychologically to occupy second place. By our teen years we've been taught to wear smiles that advertise deference. Some women smile constantly to cover an almost bottomless rage. Most of us smile inappropriately some of the time, particularly when we are angry or frightened but don't know what to do about it. We often smile at strangers, fellow employees, children, neighbors and so forth out of nervous habit. We would defend ourselves by saying we are friendly, but in fact we are afraid *not* to smile.

This habit is self-defeating. If you make your argument while beaming at your opponent you neutralize it. When you know what you have to say isn't popular and put on a big apologetic smile you convey ambivalence or appeasement. You might as well keep quiet because a gesture of submission negates the force of your words.

Far worse than the apologetic smile is the mirthless sound that punctuates many women's talk. It isn't really giggling or laughing although it sounds vaguely like it. A compulsive giggle is an apology—an apology for speaking and an apology for existing. Like insincere smiling, fake laughing signals "Don't hurt me, I'll back down."

What do women fear in these situations? We're afraid that we will be considered humorless or a bad sport. In the first place being a "good sport" is a one-down position. A good sport about what? An inordinate amount of what passes for humor is in fact strategic ridicule of women (Jewish Princess jokes, bimbo jokes and so on). As writer Evelyn Oppenheimer put it, "The oldest jokes in the world are about women and their constant chatter, their complacent disregard of facts and logic, and wives who talk their husbands to death."

Our ideas, projects, goals and positions are not a joke. Why then, when we present them, are we laughing?


## Strengthening Conversational Style

In common stereotype, women nag, gossip, talk too much, jabber about nothing, can't tell jokes properly, whine, don't get to the point and seldom finish what we start. But modern studies show that women have numerous assets as speakers. Contrary to popular opinion, women do not talk more than men.[1] Men not only talk more often than women, they talk at greater length[2] and interrupt other speakers far more often than women do.[3] The challenge is to keep the elements in our speech that we value and eliminate what doesn't work.

Women's talk is layered and reflects the ambiguity, complexity and ambivalence of living and being connected to others. As writer Mary Lou Shields puts it, "we have one eye on the cosmos and the other on the laundry." Our talk can be dense, rich and marked by fluid, swift connections. We are oriented toward process and our talk is open-ended and inclusive. Women encourage others by expressing appreciation, agreement and understanding. We draw those who are shy or quiet into the discussion. This is a speaking style we want to keep and build on. It makes women increasingly valuable as managers and on self-managed work teams as employers adopt new styles of participatory management.

But we must eliminate ways of talking that broadcast confusion, or which will be interpreted by others as powerlessness, insecurity, indecisiveness or a need for approval.

Here are some of the ways that we undermine our authority and our ability to persuade.

Many women qualify every statement to avoid sounding harsh. Instead, constant qualifying makes it seem as if the speaker does not know her own mind. For example:

> "I'd sort of like to explain. . . ."
> "It's kind of the way we do things around here. . . ."

Reinforcing statements with words like *just* and *really* suggests we don't expect to be taken seriously unless we add the extra emphasis.

> "It was really raining hard."
> "I'm really not in the mood."
> "I really think we should go."
> "It was just awful."
> "I just don't know what to say."

A surgeon who announced, "I really think you have a tumor and I'm just going to have to operate," would be frightening. Women have been conned into a double standard: a woman's unmodified, unqualified statement is rude, whereas the same statement from a man is perceived as straightforward and reassuring.

Exaggerated superlatives and overly dramatic speech about ordinary situations ("That is just divine . . . fantastic . . . marvelous . . .") in a frantic attempt to rouse a response from an inattentive listener backfire by undermining the speaker's credibility. Perhaps it can be amusing when entertainers talk this way but it is impossible to imagine a senator or a judge speaking flamboyantly for the very good reason that she would lose her reputation for levelheadedness.

"Tag questions" are mini-inquiries tacked onto declarations. Some are legitimate, as for example, "I've got a cold. This one smells like blueberry, doesn't it?"

However, as Robin Lakoff in *Language and Woman's Place* points out, sometimes "the speaker is perfectly certain of the truth of her assertion, and there is no danger of offense, but the tag appears anyway as an apology for making an assertion at all."[4] For example:

> "It's hard to make speeches, isn't it?"

> "We've been standing here a long time, haven't we?"

> "Ten percent unemployment is completely unacceptable, don't you think?"

Girls and women use more tag questions than boys and men.[5] When women use disclaimers and tag questions we are judged as less intelligent and knowledgeable than men who use them.[6]

Rising inflection indicates a question: "Ready?" "Ready!" We know the first is a question because the pitch of the speaker's voice rises when she says the word. The second "ready" is spoken with the pitch lower and is thus a statement. When someone uses a rising inflection for statements that wouldn't ordinarily call for it, she indicates uncertainty. Women often do this unconsciously. We have built "if it's all right with you?" into our speech personality.

> "What time is your friend coming over?"
> "Three o'clock?"
>
> "What are you going to do today?"
> "Oh, clean the house?"

This habit is particularly unsettling when the statement is unassailable:

> "What is your name?"
> "Janet Stone?"

We suggest insecurity when we hedge our statements, ending them with "... wasn't that right?" or "... okay?" or "... don't you agree?" or "... right?," using self-effacing diminutives ("I have a few little ideas"), and modifying firm opinions with "I guess" or "I suppose."

An addiction to passive construction equals failure to take credit for accomplishment.

> "When Jeanie was being born" instead of
> "When I gave birth to Jeanie."
>
> "Women were given the right to vote" instead of
> "We won the right to vote."

This grammatical passivity may reflect the pressure we feel toward psychological passivity. "Lady training" compels many women to speak as if *I* were not in their vocabulary, and to evade responsibility for their actions:

> "This report was written. . . ."

"After the committee was formed. . . ."
"When the garden was planted. . . ."

The fact that she wrote the report, formed the committee and planted the garden seem to have escaped the speaker's notice. We're learning to let our syntax reflect both our successes and failures. "I lost $10,000 in the stock market," "I initiated the suit," "I did it."

"Hopefully" is the misplaced adverb of the decade. It can make the speaker seem to depend on fate rather than her own capabilities. "Hopefully, I will get up on time tomorrow." "Hopefully, I'll get in shape for the tournament."

## Confined Life Talk

Obviously, any victim, male or female, of a highly routinized, low stimulus environment may degenerate by degrees into a vapid "How was your weekend?" conversationalist. If you are dissatisfied with small talk and triviality, a public speaking text alone may not be the answer.

Women are often accused of filling the air with empty chatter. Women with young children talk about them "too much" and are "boring." Boring, we might ask, to whom? Students who are in their first year at Harvard Business School talk of little else. Are they boring? Probably not to the other MBA candidates. Certainly, some aspects of life (living with teenagers, writing your Ph.D. thesis, psychoanalysis, internships, having an operation) are understandably absorbing to those engaged in them but may leave the rest of the world cold *if you do not take care to speak effectively.*

When your listener's eyes glaze over, stop talking. You are wasting your breath. Evaluate. If you haven't found a way to make your subject matter engaging to others, read on—perhaps we can help. If you can't find any problem with what you say or how you say it, you may be in the grip of gender politics . . . again.

## Modulating Your Voice

A strong pleasant voice is the greatest asset a speaker can have. Intelligence and wit are worth nothing if they cannot be heard. A high nasal pitch will destroy the most moving sentiment. Tom Brokaw, Barbara Walters and Shirley Chisholm have slight speech impediments yet are still considered good speakers; but no speaker with a disagreeable voice quality can be considered good.

A strong voice comes in part from proper breathing. When we have students under our autocratic thumbs we can coach them at length about breathing, demonstrate proper breathing techniques and help students make slow exhalation exercises habitual. However, to read about breathing is pretty insipid business. This chapter contains just enough information to help you talk louder, project your feelings and overcome nervousness. Good breath support comes from the diaphragm, which is the muscle you feel under your lungs when you pretend to blow up a balloon. Bad posture allows your abdomen to relax. Unless your diaphragm is taut, you don't have sufficient breath support to project your voice. Keep your tummy tucked in and stand up straight. If your head is up and your shoulders are down, your chest is free to work. When you are wearing your shoulders as earrings, you're tense. Lower them, and you'll loosen up a little.

Do *not* do deep breathing just before a speech. It does not relieve tension and you may pass out. Breathing regularly and exhaling slowly, consciously and regularly, work much better.

Talking continually in a loud voice while feeling emotional stress or nervous tension (or being in the vicinity of an allergen) can lead to hoarseness. The throat tightens, which strains the vocal chords. Consciously relax your throat and depend on your diaphragm for volume. Clearing your throat repeatedly will only aggravate hoarseness.

*With this posture, these arms, it will be amazing if our friend can project her voice more than a couple of feet. Furthermore, she is sure to sound tired and depressed.*

## Lowering Pitch

If you sound like a giddy little girl, you will be treated like one. A very high pitch says, "Don't expect too much of me. I am not a full-grown woman." Many of us have learned to use high-pitched kittenish voices as an appeal that as much as says, Don't hurt me. High pitch is the one vocal signature always associated with childish or immature speech.

Unfortunately, even those of us who normally speak in the

lower range of our vocal register sometimes raise our pitch on emphasis words (adjectives, adverbs, words at the end of sentences). This makes us sound frustrated and helpless. When your pitch goes down for emphasis you sound serious. Listen to your self say angrily, "I hate you!" A high pitch on *hate* will sound less convincing than a lower pitch.

It is not difficult to lower your pitch if you think it is too high. First, relax your throat muscles. Then, just for practice, groan a few times. Now repeat a word (such as *power*) in a lower pitch each time you say it until you've reached the lowest pitch you can manage. How does it sound? Would you be able to talk that low in public without cracking up? If not, try a slightly higher pitch.

If you doubt the value of retraining your everyday habits so you use a somewhat lower pitch, especially for emphasis words, try saying these sentences in a high pitch and then a low one:

> "I *defy* you to produce the evidence."
> "No, I *refuse* to accommodate that request."
> "Children, it's *important* for me to get some rest."

The point is that pitch is mostly affectation. It is true that the size of vocal chords varies and women and children generally speak in a higher pitch than men. However, the range any individual can speak in is enormous and mostly a matter of social expectation. A low pitch carries conviction and authority, which is why women should make every attempt to speak in strong, low tones.

## Correcting Nasality

Talking through your nose makes everything you say sound complaining and disagreeable. A nasal sound lacks chest resonance. Nasality can result from general physical tension, especially in the jaw and tongue, which tenses and stays high in the mouth. When the jaw is clenched all sound twangs out the nose. Regional accents often aggravate a nasal sound. The only sounds that should resonate in the head and throat are the *m, n* and *g* sounds.

To correct nasality, open everything up. Yawn and feel how throat muscles open. When you talk open your mouth *much wider* and unclench your jaw. Once you open vocal passages you should feel a stronger vibration in your chest when you talk and less vibration in your nose. Put one hand on your chest and the other on the bridge of your nose to see where the vibration originates.

High whining nasal noises are frequently made by those who feel powerless (including children) and are trying to make a stronger person pay attention. It's hard to imagine a more counter-productive approach. If you find that your pitch is high and you talk through your nose when you are almost hysterical with frustration, then changing your speech habits is only a small portion of the remedy.

Self-limiting behavior does contribute to feelings of inadequacy and allows others to perceive you as inferior. You won't become powerful just because you lower your pitch or stop playing with your hair—the condition of women is more complicated than that—but sounding stronger makes you feel stronger, and that is a good start.

## Increasing Volume

If nobody can hear you, you can't be held accountable for what you say. Low volume not only suggests low energy, low enthusiasm and weariness, it also suggests powerlessness.

In our experience the "strident" woman, although common in fiction, is very rare in real life. Despite the myths about brassy women, we find that our most difficult job is helping students stop murmuring and whispering. You must talk louder. The physical force speaking up requires, the muscle control it takes to shout, provides a psychological lift and makes you feel strong. It is no accident that yelling is an integral part of self-defense training. It makes sense. A little soft teensy voice makes you feel little, soft and teensy. A strong voice helps you feel strong.

While it is true that men dominate through interrupting or responding minimally to our remarks, we needn't collude in our own exclusion. A woman who complains, "Nobody listens to me," or "I am never recognized in meetings," or "People interrupt me all the time," is often a whisperer. If the mutterer, mumbler and end-of-sentence-dropper thinks back, she may discover that the person who routinely cuts her off today is a person who grew weary of saying, "Speak up, I didn't hear you." "What?" "Huh?" Eventually people will stop trying to hear.

When you speak to a group, remember that the folks in the back row have just as much right to hear what you have to say as those in front.

Volume comes from breath support in the abdomen and not from tight throat muscles. A taut neck with veins and cords standing out causes screeching. If you force your voice you will lose it.

## Using Words Effectively

The only foolproof way to use the best words is to write the presentation ahead of time and stick to your prepared text. But what about situations where you can't write out everything you are going to say—an interview, for example, or just an ordinary conversation? Our advice about words cannot be followed to the letter, but can serve as a general guideline. If we took the care we would have to take in order never to make these mistakes in impromptu situations we would sound like robots. But in general try to avoid the following:

*Pedantic language.* A confident speaker does not deliberately talk over people's heads. Showing off is a by-product of insecurity. As Mark Twain said about Mary Baker Eddy, "She has a perfectly astonishing talent for putting words together in such a way as to make successful inquiry into their intention impossible." Instead of stooping to condescending remarks such as, "For those of you who don't know...," a confident speaker defines her terms clearly in the first place. She doesn't need to experience the thrill of patiently—oh, so patiently—explaining her meaning to the ignoramuses.

People often say things that sound ridiculous because they want to appear sophisticated or intelligent. Overly formal or "fancy" phrasing irritates your listeners. For example, to "retire for the night," "find some other mode of transportation," "partake of a slight repast" and so forth isn't nearly as effective as stating your intent in clear, simple language.

Yet what is pretentious for one person may be sincere and natural for another. The trick is to talk like you talk. If you went to Vassar or Wellesley and can't help sounding like it, you won't endear yourself to anyone by affecting defective grammar or by borrowing "ain'ts" and "gonnas." Speak in simple, direct language.

"Always" and "never" are words that start arguments. Also, try to avoid "should," "ought" and other prescriptive words. Even if you clearly include yourself in the category of those who "should," you may still sound preachy.

*Poetic, sentimental language.* If you suspect you have written purplish prose, rehearse it in front of other people to see if you can get through it without blushing or feeling awkward. If it doesn't embarrass you, and your "audio editors" agree your language isn't too flowery, then you are probably safe.

*Slang.* Slang is a secret language for insiders. Unless you are an insider, you will get it wrong. Slang also excludes anyone who isn't an insider. It also is dangerous to dabble in technical jargon that you don't fully understand. No one will feel warmer toward you because you pretend to be like them. If you are, you are. If not, so what?

*Acronyms and initials.* State an entity's full title the first time you mention it (e.g., "the Women's Army Corps, or WAC's"; "equal employment opportunity, or EEO for short"). Some of your listeners may not know what a particular acronym stands for.

*Stereotypes.* Beware of the word—or even the idea—"typical." There is no such thing as a typical foreigner, politician, preacher, conservative, Yankee, redhead, poet, farmer, Jew, homemaker or reactionary.

*Vagueness.* Do not depend on inflection alone to provide meaning if there is a chance that you will be quoted. A sentence can be read with quite a different meaning than it had when it was spoken. If the press is covering your talk, irony, jesting and indignation are better written in than communicated to listeners through inflection.

*Fillers.* Many people use words, phrases or noises when they can't think of the right word (or can't think at all). Common examples are "Uh . . . and uh . . . ummmm . . . ya'know . . . I mean. . . ." The solution to verbal tics is to say nothing. It takes discipline simply to be quiet and think when you are having difficulty but a pause reflects much more confidence than a murmur. Try to resist asking "y'know?" at the end of every sentence. Resist beginning sentences with, "Listen." Other pads to avoid include "like . . . like. . . ," "an-da . . . an-da" and "I mean, I mean to say. . . ."

*Sexist language.* Any word, phrase or style of talking that excludes women is sexist. Using male pronouns when the sex referred to isn't plain, as in "Every student should keep his notebook in his desk,'' references to God that assume God is male, or terms such as ''man hours'' will cost you credibility, rapport or votes.

*Difficult words to say.* If it is difficult for you to say ''penis'' with equanimity, then you are better off avoiding it rather than blushing or dropping your voice. If you are embarrassed, your audience will be, too.

*Clichés.* A cliché, which is an overused, overworked expression, became popular by being apt. It's a shame that ''cold as ice,'' ''heavy as lead'' and ''dry as dust'' are hackneyed because they are expressive. If nobody had ever heard those comparisons before they would be perfect.

Diane White, a columnist for the *Boston Globe,* amassed a number of clichés for one of her columns. Here are just a few:

burning issues
coming down the pike or
  around the bend
a matter of grave concern,
  sad state of affairs, crying shame
fed up to here, same old song
  and dance
seems like yesterday, a tear
  to the eye, once upon a
  time
a hotbed of ———, a
  wasteland
at that point in time, viable
  alternatives
have to go a long way to
  top

cliché-wise, anything-wise
state of decline, throes of
  death
hard on the heels, in the
  same league with
reached heights, in our lifetime, been going
  downhill
bear the brunt of, enjoy a
  heyday, leveling
  criticism
beating a dead horse
if you get my meaning
out of the darkness, pave
  the way

Don't try too hard to find dazzling metaphors and similes if what you end up with makes you sound silly. It is better to say "dead as a doornail" than "dead as a runover cat." In fact, it would be best of all simply to say "dead."

## Varying Pace, Pitch and Volume

An interesting performance is based on variety. You can vary three basic elements in your speech: pace (how fast or slowly you talk), pitch (how high or low) and volume (how loudly or softly). If you feel strongly about what you are saying and allow your feelings to show, you will be an effective speaker. Your volume, tempo and pitch will vary naturally as you become involved with what you're saying. Unfortunately, fear and distance from the audience can flatten your personality. Unless you project yourself, you will appear static and lifeless.

Ask people you talk to every day whether they consider you a fast talker or a slow one, a soft speaker or a loud one, and whether you have a high or low pitch. If the answer is "None of the above," great. You probably vary your pace, pitch and volume to suit your words.

*Pace.* There is nothing more maddening than someone who speaks too slowly. A fast, jazzy, frantic talker can make listeners nervous, but a slow speaker can make listeners seethe. Slow speakers appear to have a high regard for their own opinion. Even though there is up to a two-minute wait between phrases and it is hard to tell when they are through, they hate to be interrupted. It takes enormous arrogance to pontificate through hours of hideous exposition on one obscure point. If you think there is *any* possibility that you talk too slowly (people napping, people interrupting you often, glazed expressions), do us all a favor and speed up. Get out the old tape recorder and talk fast into it until you have improved.

If you talk too fast or speak with an accent, concentrate on pausing between phrases and ideas rather than trying to slow down the actual rhythm of what you are saying. Pauses give your listeners a chance to catch up and "process" what you have said. When we discuss cue cards we will explain how to mark them to remind yourself to speed up or slow down.

*Pitch.* See the earlier section titled "Lowering Pitch." Remember, bring your pitch down for emphasis.

*Volume.* Once you get used to talking louder, you have to learn how to vary volume while at all times speaking up. Nothing conveys emotions more effectively than a change in volume. We all have deep associations with loud and soft sounds that are easily triggered. Use them.

## Projecting Feelings

The best way to improve the vitality of your presentation is to take the risk of letting your feelings show. Projecting those feelings to an audience is hard, but when you vary your pace, pitch and volume, your emotional tone varies as well.

## Self-Evaluation

We devised this student checklist for our Speaking Up$^{SM}$ classes. Use it to assess your presentation for strengths and weaknesses.

| *Content Strengths* | *Content Detractors* |
|---|---|
| Use of humor | Non-edited talk |
| Easy to follow | Trivializing words |
| Imaginative | (sort of, little, etc.) |
| Concrete examples | Clichés |
| Visual language | Slang |
| Convincing | Fillers (y'know, like, |
| documentation | um, uh) |
| Persuasive detail | Mispronunciation |

*Content Detractors*
  Colorless
vocabulary
  Too formal
  Misuse of words

*Delivery Detractors*
Face:
  nervous
    smiling/laughing
  deadpan or severe
  contortions (scowl-
    ing, mouthing)
  listless, apathetic
Hands:
  fidgeting/fussing
  waving around
  toying with _____
  tense, clenched,
    gripping _____
Eyes:
  rolling
  floor
  one side of room
  ceiling
  contact with audience
    not sustained
Voice:
  too fast
  too slow
  sighing
  sing-song
  monotone
  nasal
  mumbling
  whispering/inaudible
  high pitch
  choppy pacing

volume drops at end
  of sentences
lacks variety in pace,
  volume
Body:
  tense, stiff
  shoulders
    hunched
  sloppy
  wiggling
Feet:
  shuffling
  shifting weight
  crossed

*Delivery/Strengths*
  Calm recovery from
    mistakes
  No apologies
  Audible
  Not too dependent
    on text
  Relaxed manner
  Willing to take risks/
    be emotional, per-
    sonally interact
    with group
  Stong posture
  Warm smile
  Direct eye contact
  Animated face
  Pleasant pitch
  Good timing
  Varied pace
  Emphatic/meaning-
    ful gestures
  Clear enunciation

## Practicing

Experience is very important, but you don't have to get all of your experience in public. You can practice out loud by yourself. You can rehearse inflection and variety of pace by reciting letters and numbers a la "Sesame Street." You can read other people's speeches out loud—the more the better. If you have never encouraged your hammy side or if it has lain dormant since you played Mr. Tooth Decay in third grade, then speaking out will seem strange to you. Experiment at first alone and safely to give yourself a chance to get used to this new dramatic voice ringing in your ears. You must be authentic, your real self—but you can gradually expand the outside limits of your capacity to draw tears or cheers.

## Getting Better

You are probably thinking that the whole thing is too much. You are right. You can't fix everything all at once; in fact, you can't fix everything, period. The point is improvement. Strengthening your speech personality is a matter of establishing priorities. Begin at the beginning and strive to attain one goal at a time. In our opinion, the basic, fundamental goals to concentrate on are as follows: standing up straight, looking people right in the eye, talking loudly and being authentic. All the rest is gravy.

A final thought about being authentic. A good speaker often must be willing to sacrifice "perfect" delivery in order to be genuine. We like and identify with some speakers and not others. We believe some speakers and not others. The difference isn't their technical competence at speech making. If you respect your audience and care about what you are saying and if you are willing to risk exposing your real self, then you will have less trouble establishing rapport—and recovering calmly from your errors. It is common sense. It is probably what you have been telling yourself all along.

If your real issue is fear, read on.

# CHAPTER THREE

# Nerves

*"I am at the boiling point! If I do not find some day the use of my tongue ... I shall die of an intellectual repression, a women's rights convulsion."*
—Elizabeth Cady Stanton in a letter to Susan B. Anthony

Although only one of our students has ever said right out loud, "I want to make myself invisible," many have acted as if being inconspicuous is an ideal. Our subordinate status is reflected in and perpetuated by behavioral norms that continue to tell women to keep quiet, to hold back, to let someone else take the credit, to be diplomatic, to be sorry. These limits directly contradict what a speaker tries to do behind a podium. We've spent a lot of time in our workshops trying to pinpoint exactly what our students are afraid of. Over the years it has become clear that deep down inside they fear the penalties for breaking the rules they have internalized for behavior that is "appropriate" for women.

It is very frightening to stand up in front of people who don't have to reveal whether they agree or not, and don't have to say whether they like you or not, if all your life you have sought immediate and constant reassurance. Most people don't like conflict (especially open conflict); many women have had to make "don't be mad at me" their motto.

Some of us have arranged our lives to avoid situations in which even the possibility of failure would arise. We put off testing ourselves and live on fantasies of what we will do, or might do or could do next month, next year or if we felt like it. No wonder we are afraid. We don't have a realistic idea of our ability, of what failure feels like or know whether we can take the heat.

The following four limitations (which we emphasize when treating a student's nervousness) are products of women's subordinate status in power relations in our culture.

- *Lack of self-knowledge.* If your range of options was stunted from the early years, a career counselor's standard questionnaire about likes and dislikes, strengths and weaknesses, potential and underutilized ability is almost useless. The answer to many questions will be "I don't know." Self-awareness for women still gets equated with "selfishness" (except for acute awareness of pimples, pounds and gray hair).

- *Lack of practice.* It's hard to tell whether you are potentially capable of public speaking or whether you will enjoy it if you only get to try once a year.

- *Lack of role models.* Until recently there were precious few women on the lecture circuit, in the boardrooms or on the six o'clock news. That made it hard for many of us to feel entitled to step up to the mike, and when we did, it was hard to know what traits or styles might be good to emulate. Without models to observe and learn from, many women more or less taught themselves speaking skills.

- *Lack of approval for growing stronger.* Friends, colleagues and bosses sometimes react with uneasiness when a Speaking Up$^{SM}$ course starts to "take." Your fledgling confidence can be undermined by people who are threatened by this new you. They may say things to try to keep you from changing. If speaking your mind or assuming leadership is met with disapproval, try to resist the rationalization that you didn't want to do it anyway.

## Avoiding Bonding Through Failure

What estranges you from one group of people might endear you to another. "Friends" who offer you acceptance on the basis of your weaknesses are not helping you.

It is a psychological truism that a partner in a relationship all too often is not patiently suffering from the other partner's dependence or shortcoming; he or she is counting on it.

If you and your friend are teamed up to bolster each other's weakening resolve to finish a degree program, the one who says, "This is too hard, let's drop out," invites a deadly togetherness. It is too easy to fall back on the feeling that your ambitions for yourself aren't really important, anyway. Reinforcement of low self-esteem in women is socially acceptable. Few object to the woman who doesn't speak up, who doesn't make speeches. In fact, you'll probably encounter resentment when you refuse to collude with "Let's don't try" offers of intimacy.

When you establish your friendships on the basis of support and mutual strengthening, rather than the comfort of giving up together, difficult tasks become progressively easier. This is part of our strategy in forming classes on a peer group basis. The students bring to the class varying degrees of nervousness, but they understand that a precondition of their registration is helping one another push through the anxiety when it feels like quitting time.

Then there is the pseudo-support most common in marriages. A woman might say, "Gee, I'm really scared about the report I have to give tomorrow." The mate who replies "Then why don't you call in sick?," or, "You'll be fine, honey," without looking up from the newspaper displays a sort of "helpfulness" that is only an obstacle.

Those who may try to hold you back (usually in far more subtle ways than the ones mentioned here) are often the very people whose support you count on the most: parents, a lover, a best friend or a boss.

Women often say, "I'm all right if the group is just women, but I really clutch if the audience is mostly men." A woman who isn't nervous when there are "just" women may feel that she doesn't count somehow and therefore that the opinions of other women ("just the girls") don't count either. Or, her experience with mixed sex groups may have taught her that her opinions will be over-scrutinized and picked to death by colleagues who undermine her.

Of course, it is reasonable to be particularly nervous about the response of those who have power over you. Working women whose salary and promotions depend on a boss's sponsorship suffer realistic conflicts about speaking up. A boss may extend approval to subordinates who smile a lot, who rush to say a lot of nothing to camouflage the serious intent of an assertive statement or who delight in being smart, but never as smart as he is. Sometimes obsequiousness works in the short run. In the long run, it fails, leaving the fawner bitter and without the skills she could have been developing.

We've all been ignored when we do well, ridiculed when we fail, made to feel different and out of place when we are finally included. But even if the results of your risks are the unfortunate possibilities you dread, remember that the alternative wasn't so hot, either. "Troublemaker" can be a nasty name for "pioneer," and "failure" can be a nasty name for "seasoning."

## Solving the Nervousness Problem

Only the speaker who doesn't care doesn't feel anything. Emotional reactions to an audience can be excitement, a buzz of anticipation, a slightly "up" feeling, a tingle. You are at your physical and mental best when you are keyed up. You don't do your best at a task you don't regard as sufficient challenge to cause mild anxiety. When a seasoned performer loses her "good nerves," when she looks at a speech as a routine job, her relationship with the audience is jeopardized. We promise that if you speak in public often enough you will eventually know what it means to *miss* that feeling of intensity.

Unfortunately, your emotional reaction to an audience can also be panic. There is a tremendous difference between the excitement that motivates an effort and stage fright. The physical manifestations are similar or identical (e.g., perspiration, tremors). But genuine stage fright is so unpleasant that many of us sacrifice our careers or personal potential to avoid experiencing it.

Sometimes stage fright feels like shell shock. Your ears buzz. It is hard to remember ordinary things, to interpret reactions, to understand what's going on. You feel shaky, numb, "out of it." In this condition you have to take particular care to orient yourself, to ground yourself and avoid strange behavior. You're susceptible to guffawing wildly or walking into a closet. Fear may cause joyless laughter, breathing difficulty, foot jiggling, dry mouth, wishing you were dead and other common symptoms.

No matter how frightened you are, remember the audience is just people. A speech is just talking. There is no real physical threat. The novice will do well to allow a molehill to remain a molehill. Stage fright is not fatal.

## Deciding to Overcome Fear

> *"I am glad to have lived fully in the main current of my times, making some effort to grapple with our most vital problems."*
> —Virginia Gildersleeve,
> Dean of Barnard

We cannot guarantee you will completely lose your stage fright—there are always new audiences and new challenges that can trigger it ("What on earth is *mother* doing here?"). However, we can offer suggestions to control stage fright, to turn it into a keen edge that will help you. Most students say that they are happier when they learn to hide the obvious signs of their fright so well that others don't detect them, even though the fear itself remains.

Don't allow fear to be an excuse. Since childhood you've developed the mechanics of overcoming fear and by going through the motions over and over again you have become strong at all kinds of things that used to scare you. And, you already know that when you avoid situations in which you have to use your brains and guts, you reinforce cowardice.

Everyone begins as a beginner. "All great speakers," says Ralph Waldo Emerson, "were bad speakers first." The fact that others speak "better" than you do is irrelevant. You, too, will be better the second time than you were the first. The fact that you still won't be perfect the second time, or the tenth, is what we call "life." Get used to it.

You have noticed that the people who achieve are not necessarily the ones with the most ability. Those who "make it" are the ones who decide to use what ability they have, the ones who conquer their fear. Decide you will not let your fear push you around or make your decisions for you. Psychologists call our advice "reaction formation." That sappy Rodgers and Hammerstein song, "Whenever I feel afraid, I hold my head erect and whistle a happy tune so no one will suspect I'm afraid," is actually a million-dollar strategy.

If we knew some way to get around the necessity for visibility in building a career, we'd tell you about it. If we knew a magic formula to release a flow of brilliant, clear and fitting language for each occasion, especially the difficult early ones, we would reveal it. The fact is we all learn by doing. Maybe it will be easy and your improvement will be rapid. Or you may adapt slowly, through failure and error.

A hundred years ago people likely to end up in responsible positions (upper-class men) went through extensive public speaking training. Nowadays, most of us have to get "on-the-job" training.

In short, if you believe you can't possibly do it, you'll never give yourself a chance. You have to speak in order to learn to speak well. There are shortcuts, like reading this book and taking workshops. But the irreducible minimum, the nonnegotiable inevitable, is hauling your terrified self to the spotlight and quaking in it until you improve.

## I'm Afraid I'll Make a Mistake

The question is not how to avoid mistakes or nervous symptoms completely. You can't. Unfortunate things do happen. The question is how to plan so that you will make fewer mistakes and so that when you do make them you recover.

Great stars plan "mistakes." They think human frailty makes them more accessible to the audience and they're right. Of course, that's poor comfort to the rest of us who would rather be a little less human at this stage. But you can learn something from the idea of planning mistakes. It is easy to take a planned pratfall with charm and humor. If you aren't ready to plan your mistakes, at least you can decide what to do about the mistakes you are likely to make. Planning is the opposite of worrying.

We take a strict problem-solving approach to nerves in our classes. Students are asked to think about the specific errors or nervous symptoms they fear, and then devise a concrete strategy to deal with each of them. The embarrassments haunting your imagination actually happen to people. You cannot prevent everything. But you can recover.

One good way to counter a phobia is to give it its due. The things we fear are not silly if they stop us from trying. Here is the key: an audience will overlook or forget almost any horror if you allow them to. Adequate preparation and a recovery plan will carry you through to triumph. Later, only you, your speech teacher and your mother will remember that your presentation wasn't perfect.

## Addressing Common Fears

Throughout this section we will give you answers to the question "What if . . . ?" All the answers have something in common. It doesn't matter what happens. What matters is your attitude toward what happens. That attitude should be unapologetic, good-humored, self-accepting and cool.

You may think your secret fear is original, but we bet it isn't. There are only so many ghastly possibilities. These are some common fears:

> Not being able to start speaking, standing there mute
> Having the audience laugh at you
> Losing your train of thought, going blank
> Voice shaking and cracking
> Hands shaking, knees knocking, legs trembling
> Diarrhea
> Vomiting
> Sweating profusely
> Fainting
> Boring the audience to sleep
> Tripping, falling down, walking into walls, dropping notes
> Crying
> Blushing
> Stomach rumbling, belching, farting, wetting your pants
> False teeth coming loose, glasses getting broken, wig falling off
> Saying some horrible faux pas, babbling incoherently
> Mispronouncing words
> Coprolalia (uncontrollable outburst of obscenity)

We won't address every anxiety on the list (and maybe your secret nightmare isn't even on it). The fundamental strategy remains the same in *every* case. You're standing there "with your face hanging out," as they say in television, with a choice.

You can pull yourself together or you can come unstuck. Depending on what you do, the audience will either refocus quickly on your ideas or be forced to fixate on your disaster.

Retaining the appearance of calm is half the secret to recovering calm. "Retaining the appearance of calm" means that you stop at one mistake. Instead of recovering according to a plan, we tend to let symptoms pile up in sequence until we feel overpowered by them (e.g., first the burp, which leads to wiggling and pawing the ground with your feet and to rising pitch, and so on). You are going to stop at the first glitch, relax, stay cool and forget it.

*Getting sick.* If your stomach tends to go wild under stress, we can assume a speech will generate more than enough stress to upset it. Be prepared. If you get diarrhea, don't eat much ahead of time, take a prescribed amount of an over-the-counter antidiarrhea medicine and bring more with you to the talk. If vomiting is your stomach's preferred mode of self-expression, ask your doctor to prescribe an antinausea drug. Then arrange to have a trash can off stage (no, we're not kidding) in case the women's room is a hundred yards from the podium. Include an airline vomit bag in your notebook or briefcase.

Although nausea usually can be controlled through slow exhalation breathing, it is comforting to have an emergency plan. When you arrive at the site of your talk, find out where the nearest bathroom is and figure out the fastest route to it. If you get sick after you've already started your briefing, remember the audience will act like an audience—passive, willing to accept whatever expectations you set up for them provided you seem to know what you are doing. Excuse yourself with aplomb, say you will be right back, smile and make a dash for it. If you don't act like it's a big deal, they will just sit there and wait for you to come back. Livelier audiences will begin talking amongst themselves. Work groups will move on to something else.

Your backward body is waging guerrilla warfare against you.

Your body is a tool of your antediluvian subconscious; it still believes that it isn't nice for girls to make speeches. Think of your body as a sweet but old-fashioned relative. It will come around eventually if you are firm.

If you are appearing on radio or television the moves are exactly the same. "I have to leave the set now, Oprah; I'll be back later in the show to answer a few more questions." Smile, exit, run. The host of the show is a trained professional; she or he knows what to do next and if she can't roll with the punches and ad lib, that isn't your problem. When Sally Quinn was doing the "Good Morning America" program she worried about having an "accident." A colleague told her about Walter Cronkite's professionalism carrying him gamely through an on-air attack of diarrhea. It wasn't a true story, but it could have been.

*The shakes.* One thing you can do to practically guarantee trembling is to go all rigid and refuse to move in any direction. We recommend that you get out there on those watery legs and stride around. Release your grip on the podium, bend your knees a little, move your arms, use your muscles. If you lock your body in a single pose, your shaking can only grow more vigorous.

We think shaking is intriguing because although it is painfully obvious to the speaker, it often cannot be detected by the audience. Time and again in our workshops a participant will confess that she thought her body would fly apart from trembling during her speech and her audience will be amazed and disbelieving. She looked fine to them. The shakes are disruptive only if you allow them to distract you; they are inconspicuous to others.

Index cards and heavy paper stock rattle less in fear-palsied hands. Avoid noisy bracelets and wear safe shoes (when your legs turn to jelly, spike heels are a menace).

A shaking voice demands more sophisticated planning because this symptom *is* noticeable. First, get rid of all the distracting apologetic gestures you've developed to go with the voice. (For most of us these are conspicuous swallowing, grimacing and head shaking.) Again, recovery consists of refusing to compound your troubles by drawing more agonizing attention to your errors and to your feelings of humiliation. Continue to make strong eye contact. Next, pull in your stomach, increase your volume slightly, and lower your pitch. Do not inhale more air than you need to say your next phrase or sentence. If you do, you will wind up sighing out the excess or choking it back. A huge gulp of air escapes when your speak, causing you to sound squeaking, reedy and quivering. Too much inhaled air is also the cause of the panting and the jerky cadences that accompany a wobbly voice.

Tense facial muscles may tremble, too. Again, the symptom disconcerts the speaker but is seldom observed by the audience. Before going "on," hide in a private place and make faces. Blow up your cheeks. This is what television people do to relax a taut, rigid expression. If your facial twitches prevent you from smiling naturally, don't smile. Look interested instead, and just keep talking. You can convey welcome, interest or pleasure without baring your teeth.

*Blushing.* It takes grit to stand there blushing and sweating yourself into cardiac arrest. It isn't easy to ignore the accompanying pulsing sensations and pretend you don't feel like a bonfire. However, if you concentrate on your remarks and resist the impulse to complement the blush with adolescent moves like shrugging or rolling your eyes, you not only will have overcome your problem but you will look better than the rest of us. Even short distances have a way of wiping out detail. Office lights, never mind stage lights, make most Caucasians look ill. A nice healthy blush will help compensate for lights and make you look terrific to row three and beyond. It may be torture for you, but by now you can tell that we agree with Dorothy Sarnoff, author of *Speech Can Change Your Life.* "Shyness," she says, "is I-ness." Blushing is an excellent example of speaker misery that should not be shared with your audience. Speaking isn't *about* you; it is *for* them.

*Hot flashes.*   A woman who is going through a difficult menopause and knows she may be subject to a hot flash should bring along several strong cotton handkerchiefs. Trying to mop a good flash with a tissue is silly. You're left holding a ratty-looking damp little wad. Handkerchiefs are better. The same thing goes for crying, by the way. Many of us have been made to feel ashamed of crying the same way we've been made to feel ashamed of menstruating or ceasing to menstruate or being hugely pregnant or other "crimes." Phooey. We are women. Sometimes we stifle crying, sometimes not. That's that. Take a handkerchief and get on with it.

*Going blank.*   When speaking impromptu or using an outline, it is common for a speaker to forget a word she wants to use. Stop and visualize what you are trying to describe if it's concrete; the word may pop out as soon as the picture forms in your head. If the word doesn't materialize, go ahead cheerfully with your talk. "... It's ah, ah ... you know, ah ... I don't know why I can't think of it, it's right on the tip of my tongue, damn, what is that word anyway ...?" and so forth is just excruciating.

Our concept of time gets a little warped in front of a crowd. If you have been winging it successfully up to the point where you go blank, remember that it only takes a moment or two of interruption to find your place in your notes; the pause is far better than babbling.

You may go blank about your whole subject, although this happens mostly in our nightmares, rarely in reality. (In fact, considering what we do say sometimes under stress, we often wish we had gone blank.) Like throwing up, going blank could be your subconscious mind's revenge. You go blank because you don't want to say whatever it is that you had planned to say. Maybe you are afraid the audience won't like it, or your father wouldn't like it, or who knows what. Always carry some notes, however minimal, so that you can't cop out that way. Take your notes to the podium with you even if you don't think you will use them. The time you go blank may be the hundredth time you describe how to install the system. We stress preparation and adequate notes precisely because it eliminates one more excuse. "Losing the train of thought" is an unnecessary worry. If worse comes to worst, you can just read your notes out loud. Nobody will be impressed with your skill as a speaker but you will have delivered your message.

If you have absolutely no time to prepare and go completely blank, smile and say, "I have gone completely blank."

*Saying the wrong thing—bloopers.* From a statement by Lieutenant General Patrick F. Cassidy in the Fort Riley, Kansas, *Post,* as quoted in *The New Yorker:*

> I express to all men and women of the Fifth Army my heartiest congratulations. For the first time since 1947 our Army is free of the draft. We are moving rapidly as a professional force. The Active Army, Army National Guard and Army Reserve are now molded together as a team engaged in the struggle for the prevention of peace.

When you make a funny mistake, people laugh. It is not derisive or mocking laughter, but simple human enjoyment of something amusing. We usually say the wrong thing right smack in the middle of the most sensitive part of the speech. That makes it hard for us to join in the laughter, but join in if you can. Don't try to start again until you are sure the merriment has thoroughly died down.

If you do mispronounce a word, say words in the wrong order, begin to deliver page six before you have delivered page five, or inadvertently say the word that means the opposite of what you intend to say then stop. Fall silent. Make the correction and move on. For example: "The dorbal of the farm . . .

*When you make a mistake, don't telegraph it.*

the *or-deal* of the farm worker. . . ." Don't bother to apologize, just stop and start over, eyes up, using strong emphasis and inflection to make the correction. Skip the correction altogether if you're pretty sure the word will be clear from the context. Radio and television announcers slur words frequently but just sail right along.

If you totally screw up your script, make nonsense of a sentence, or take your ideas out of order and render them incomprehensible, you will have to explain. The audience deserves to know that *they* haven't suddenly lost touch with reality; it's you. Don't apologize ("I'm doing this poorly"); just do it again more clearly: "I'm going to go over that again—it wasn't clear."

When you repeat something correctly, keep your eyes up. We have all seen a speaker reread a section of a speech she has blown, head nodding over the text, shoulders hunched over, nose practically in her notes. "Yep," she seems to be saying, "that's what it says all right." This makes her look goofy; she did write the speech after all.

*Waking a bored audience.*  You begin a presentation aflame with enthusiasm, ready to be carried out on the shoulders of the crowd amid shouts of thunderous approval. Five minutes into the speech and you'll settle for no booing. As comic Joan Rivers would say, you're playing to "tired air." This happens to *everyone.*

Performers say things like, "You're a great audience," because there are rotten terrible sleepy audiences who wouldn't wake up if you offered cash prizes. When members of the audience yawn, read their programs, gaze out the window, snore audibly or get up and walk out, it is very upsetting. The worst thing you can do is to fall into a monotone muttering delivery as a way of pretending you're not there.

A bored audience calls for more risk taking, not less. Find two or three responsive, sympathetic faces and look to them for reinforcement. Play to them until your voice, your posture, your overall manner is jacked up. Care about them, communicate with them and use their positive feedback. If you can't find two sympathetic faces just do it for yourself. Since they don't seem to care anyway, think of it as a dress rehearsal and really work on polishing your performance. *What have you got to lose?*

Try to avoid getting strained and desperate. If it is hopeless and nothing you try seems to help, cut short the formal part of your presentation and move to the question-and-answer period. Sometimes apathy is disguised hostility and things liven up when you give the audience a chance to explain why they hate you. If there aren't even any questions, then just stop. A dead horse is a dead horse. This happens to everyone at one time or another, and although it is unnerving, we survive and live to tell the tale to comfort younger, less experienced speakers.

If you informed three or four people with your presentation but left the rest cold, it was not a failure. It is sufficient to be able to say with pride that you connected with a few of those who heard you talk. It's not easy to persuade people.

Even if you are a great speaker who is having a "hot" day with a dynamite talk, you will still miss about 20 percent of your audience. Some of the faces in front of you are unreachable. He is focused on his ulcer, she on her accountant's grim report. They are contemplating their impending divorces or worrying about flatulence, and nothing will tempt them to listen.

*Inelegance.*   What do you do about burping, coughing, sneezing, a runny nose and itching? Say, "Excuse me," cover your mouth, blow and scratch, in that order. Do it vigorously, get it over with. You call unnecessary attention to these distractions by trying to be subtle with them. Nothing is more aggravating than little throat clearings and teensy sniffles that go on and on and never do the job.

Throat clearing is often a nervous gesture, a habit, a stall. If you have a sinus condition, you probably already have a prescription for a nasal spray or decongestant. Always have a glass of water at hand. Avoid milk, beer, ice cream and grape juice on the day of the presentation, and, obviously, steer clear of carbonated beverages.

*Sweat.*   We know an ex-homecoming queen who defied the South Carolina heat by spraying antiperspirant all over her face before an "important" dance, but we do not recommend this technique. We do recommend large cotton handkerchiefs used with no apology. Mousy, surreptitious dabbing only makes you appear self-conscious when, in Woody Allen's fine phrase, you are "perspiring audibly." Swamp Thing underarms can be taken care of by a trip to the dime store where dress shields still sell cheaply.

*Dry mouth.* Fear causes dry mouth. So does a lot of smiling—even your teeth can dry off. A dry mouth makes a peculiar smacking sound, which can be distracting, especially if you are on a mike. Abrade your tongue against your teeth to make saliva flow. Some speakers stick a tiny sharp-flavored cinnamon candy under their tongues. Ask for water at the podium and drink it when you need to. If your body is so rigid that pouring and drinking water makes you spastic, you aren't moving around naturally enough in the first place. To keep their smiles from sticking at the gumline, pageant contestants rub a thin smear of Vaseline across their teeth. Don't experiment with something weird like this without first trying it at home.

*Major klutziness.* What if you trip, fall, drop your cue cards, knock the lectern off the table or walk into the flip chart? By now you must know the answer. The worse the mistake, the more important it is to maintain composure. If you want the audience to forget it happened you must carry on without fuss. It is your *job* to spare the audience discomfort by not betraying your own.

If a heel breaks as you cross the stage, remove both shoes and advance to the podium. If you knock your glasses off the podium and they skitter six feet down the aisle and under someone's chair, you say, "I can't deliver my prepared speech without glasses because I can't see," and go pick them up. Cope!

Of course, your first reaction is simply to lie down and die. Unfortunately, no matter how long you lie there, the morgue won't come for you. You must go on, and you owe the audience something. They didn't come to see you fall down, after all, and while it was momentarily amusing they still expect to hear you talk. Talk! Later, after you get home, you can obsess, agonize, hate yourself, cry and bore your family and friends to death. Much later, after you've gotten your ego on a leash and regained your perspective, you'll regard the debacle as a "training speech." Later still, you will employ the entire episode as fodder for your legend.

## Avoid Apologies

Never apologize to someone unless you have injured her. Do not yell "Whoops!" or say "Oy, I just can't get it together today" or "Gee, I sure am a mess here." Do not smack your forehead in dismay, shake your head, rattle your papers, shift from foot to foot, squirm or wave your hands in agitation. What is the point of apologizing, verbally or nonverbally, for your shortcomings? To whom are you apologizing? No one is hurt because you forgot a word, mixed up your cards, broke into a sweat and tripped over a chair on your way out. Certainly, no one is injured if you were good, but not as brilliant as you hoped and expected. It is very hard to stop saying "excuse me, I'm sorry, forgive me, please, I beg your pardon. . . ." We're sorry to be fat, sorry to be thin, sorry to be mothers, sorry to be Republicans, sorry to be gay, communists, antivivisectionists and gardeners. We're sorry we're so clumsy, and thirty-five, and conventional, and different, and talk too much, and not enough and sorry we can't disappear altogether. If you don't believe it, stop apologizing for one day. Forbid yourself even so much as a self-deprecating shrug. You'll see how hard it is.

There is silence after you make a statement and let it stand. There is silence after you forget your next word. Most of us can't bear that silence so we fill it up with apology. Learn how to live with that silence and you will have learned almost everything you need to know about self-confidence.

## How to Relax

Adequate preparation usually takes the edge off all but the most vicious cases of nervous tension. We also want to recommend a few tranquilizing exercises.

*Offstage relaxers.* The time finally arrives when there is, as you sigh to yourself, "Nothing left to do except brace myself

*She is not smiling at something funny. She is saying, "Please like me, I'm harmless."*

and go ahead with it." If you are offstage, in a radio studio, in the interviewer's anteroom or otherwise out of sight, sneak in a series of neck rolls.

Or, from a standing position, bend over slowly from the waist to allow your head and arms to dangle loosely toward the floor. Waggle your fingers. Slowly sway as though sweeping the floor with your hands. Keep your neck relaxed by letting your head drop completely.

One caveat: Know yourself—neck rolls aren't for everyone.

If you are not in shape, don't just flop over suddenly. You may never straighten up again. Those of us with bum spines have to approach this sort of thing gingerly.

*Onstage relaxers.*   Check your hands for stage fright. Many of us clench our fists, wring our hands nervously (especially if they are cold from fear) or get white knuckles from grasping the podium or the arm of a chair. To calm yourself, allow your hands to fold into a limp pose in your lap, or if you are standing, allow them to hang loosely at your sides. It's very difficult to keep your hands limp and loose when you are nervous, but more important, it's hard to remain tense if your hands are relaxed.

Generally, keep moving but don't wiggle. A deliberate change of position from time to time will keep your blood circulating, prevent your hands and feet from turning to ice and make you feel more "normal." Wiggling, on the other hand, makes you feel childish and look worse. If you must cross one leg over the other, don't swing it. Avoid twirling your ankles in circles.

*Diverting tension.* It's great to play cat, to stretch and yawn, or to play scarecrow and swing your arms loosely around as though they were being flipped in the breeze. These exercises are guaranteed to make you feel better. But you can't do them in front of the sales management team. Suppressed finger tapping or nail biting will seek some other outlet. We recommend that you find an inconspicuous way to let your body express tension as a stopgap measure until you no longer feel especially nervous about public speaking. This "Plan a Tic" strategy allows you to work out your feelings in a minimally disruptive way; you can both release the nervousness and look your best.

There are several methods that will permit your body to let off steam, less obtrusively than, say, compulsively adjusting your bra strap. Your nervous habit should be appropriate on a stage or in meetings when people are looking at you. You can use slow exhalation breathing when you are being observed. You also can concentrate your nervous energy into one part of your body.

Experiment with pressing your thumb hard up against the side of the index finger next to it. Leave the rest of your fingers curling around naturally. One white thumb knuckle will show. In the meantime, your face is composed, your posture is erect and your mind is trained on whatever is happening in the group. This technique is a counterirritant. The principle is the same when you pinch yourself on the arm when the dentist's drill is whining.

Some people dig one fingernail into the palm of the same hand. Others curl up the toes on one foot, confining muscular tensions to one spot. You can pinch your earlobe with great force without hurting it or calling attention to yourself while you are seated at a desk or table. Yet this pressure gives your body a chance to let its nervousness "talk."

## How Not to Relax

*Don't drink.* You know that. We know that. The ferrets in the far north know that. Alcohol doesn't work. A drink will fuddle your brain, your tongue, your vision and your balance. It will not steady your nerves. The combination of alcohol and adrenaline in your system can have unexpected and unpleasant side effects (like hives; this is not cute). Coffee will not sober you up. It only produces an awake drunk person, as any state trooper will attest.

If you are drinking anything stronger than water your liaison will worry that you may turn out like their speaker from three years ago, who was plastered by the time she was introduced. Your hosts want you to do well. Don't cause them unnecessary edginess by trying to dull your panic at the bar.

When the speaker joins the group in a cocktail at the pre-speech banquet, the group isn't consciously disapproving. In fact, if you ask, most people will look puzzled or claim to *prefer* that their speaker "has a little knock before she has to work, har har." There is usually, however, a silent undercurrent of expectation that you abstain. Water is the best drink. A carbonated beverage may bring on burping. If you are eating lightly before the speech, coffee can make you sick. Caffeine may stimulate you more than it usually does; combined with an oversupply of adrenaline it can give you an unpleasant "racy" feeling.

*Lay off the pills.* Your first stand-up presentation is the wrong time to begin experimenting with mood altering substances. Even if you have a prescription for a mild tranquilizer and you know how it affects you, it still may be better to make friends with your "belly moths" rather than chemically annihilate them. Depend on yourself to avoid and recover from the symptoms of stage fright. Can you imagine anything more boring than a tranquil speaker?

# Summary

To relax for a speech, to feel mentally ready and loose, requires about 90 percent preparation, and 10 percent everything else: breathing technique, relaxation exercises, recovery strategies and psyching yourself. Pills and booze rate 0 percent. You calm yourself best by relying on adequate preparation. Give yourself every edge, do yourself every favor, allow yourself every break. Don't saddle yourself with any concerns beyond the speech itself. Make sure you are *ready.*

When you have done all the constructive symptom-solving you can, forget it. Replace every anxious "What if . . ." with your fantasy of yourself as Ms. Competent of the Western Hemisphere.

Fantasize success, including successful recovery. Psych yourself by envisioning yourself doing well, turning people on, feeling your words as you say them, looking self-assured. Hear yourself speaking in your best voice—full of life, at a pleasant pitch and loud enough for all to hear. Keep this image in mind; enjoy the daydream.

Then do it. Speak up. Throw yourself vigorously into the action you fear. Do it again and again. Solicit opportunities to get experience. Never let a meeting go by without making a contribution. Practice builds confidence. The mixed feelings of fear, relief and satisfaction eventually become a genuine desire to communicate and participate. On the day you do an outstanding job you will know it and so will everyone who was listening. This is a thrill so addictive it can hook the most retiring novice. Dick Cavett, who has had plenty of opportunity to reflect on stage fright, reminds us that the gratifications (the big laugh, the rapt silence, the awesome thrill of charming the unruly beast out there) are unimaginable and unavailable at the beginning. But some day, he says, if you are determined, you will know exactly why Judy Garland, exhausted and distressed, would choose to stay on for one more song.

Reduce the general fear in your life by trying related

confidence-builders. Practice making yourself conspicuous. Walk down the aisle to sit at the front of lecture halls and movie theaters. Stay out of chairs in corners. Ask questions in big groups. Bungee jump.

> *"We must choose between the delights and pleasures of safety or growth."*
> —Abraham Maslow

# CHAPTER FOUR

---

# How to Arrange a Successful Speech

Many of the participants in Speaking Up[SM] workshops think that they have never made a "speech." They take our courses to learn to present themselves effectively in "everyday" situations. But before long it becomes clear that most of them *have* made speeches and will make many more. Whenever you give a report at a meeting, introduce a speaker, give instructions to a group, orient the newcomers, present an award or pitch an idea, you are making a presentation. The purpose of the next three chapters is to take the mystery out of making a good one. The advice is applicable to every presentation whether it is long or short, widely heard or meant for a few. We will take you through everything step by step. The steps are simple but they take a while to explain and to read. Naturally, we don't expect you to do all the "do's" or avoid the "don'ts"—nobody ever has—but we've tried to make sure that they are all here.

Many inexperienced speakers seem to believe that only "speeches" on state occasions call for careful serious preparation and notes. We cannot overemphasize how mistaken this notion is. While there are occasions on which you have to speak without preparation (impromptu) or on which you have time to think about what you want to say but no time to prepare more than a sketchy outline (extemporaneous), they should be rare. A competent performance demands preparation, rehearsal and good notes. Respect *all* your audiences, whether your presentation is at a small meeting, in a panel discussion, at an outdoor rally or to the General Assembly of the United Nations. Don't allow the size of the audience, the seriousness of the occasion or the length of the talk to determine your preparation; make full preparation every time your standard.

At first, it might seem that the first step in preparing a talk would be to write it. Not so. Before you can write an effective presentation you have to take stock. For what audience are you writing? What is the situation? What kind of speech should it be? What is the purpose of your speech? What tone do you want to take?

A briefing is an extended answer to a question. For example, talks with titles like "A Brief History of the Women's Movement in England" or "Food Cooperatives and How They Work" or "The Employee Benefit Program and How to Use It" are probably briefings. Briefings are characterized by neutrality. The speaker does not take a stance or point of view; she's not trying to "sell" the audience anything.

A persuasive talk is one that tries to get the audience to take action, to think or to do something. Your purpose is to influence attitude, behavior or policy. It is usually informative as well, but because you care about convincing your audience you invest more of your beliefs, personality, values and emotions in a persuasive presentation. You almost never tell anyone anything without also trying to get her to apply, interpret or experience the information in a certain perspective—yours.

To persuade, you must discover what motivates your audience, find out what is likely to sway them. It is not enough to inform the audience of the *features* (aspects) of a course of action. You must also describe the *benefits* of the action to those you wish to persuade. People act on your recommendations only if they think it's in their interest to do so. People will listen to almost anything if it is entertaining, but won't *do* anything unless they believe it will get them something.

You also must find out what it is that people don't want to hear, what their concerns and reservations are, what they object to, and address (not ignore) these objections in a persuasive talk.

Different audiences react to different things. The trick is to figure out what these hot buttons are. In general, people who pride themselves on being hardheaded realists (such as business people, scientists, engineers) respond to facts, while those who think of themselves as humanitarians or intuitive or good with people respect feelings as information, too.

Keep in mind that the smaller the audience, the less effective a soaring appeal to emotions will be. People in small groups feel more like individuals than members of large audiences do, and the "herd" response of a crowd to a direct appeal to feelings (sympathy, patriotism, outrage) may be missing.

All of your presentations will be better written and more interestingly presented if you care and show that you care about your subject. If you believe that your ideas and recommendations are important, that belief will be contagious. Unfortunately, new speakers are not always able to muster that self-confidence initially. It doesn't matter. Speaking out is intrinsically self-assertive, and as you learn to do it and do it effectively, your self-confidence and your faith in your own ideas grow. Eventually you may become a brilliant speaker. In the meantime, when you sit down to put together a presentation, ask yourself: "Why do I care and why should others care?"

## Ask Your Liaison Person to Help

Your contact person can be a tremendously effective ally. She (or he) not only invites, greets you (and perhaps pays you), she also can be your link to the group in other ways. You can and should use her knowledge of the group and her experience. Pose the right questions, ask for her help. She has an investment in your performance, so whether your liaison is your supervisor at work or a stranger, she will probably be more than willing to find out for you what you need to know. The following sections contain suggestions for using a liaison person's energy to your mutual advantage. You also may be a liaison person yourself from time to time; these tips will help you assist the speakers you work with to avoid unpleasant surprises and do a good job.

The length of your presentation, the complexity of the issues you present and the approach you take will depend on the answers to the following questions:

*What is the occasion for which you are gathered?* Will the general atmosphere be solemn or light? Will the audience expect instruction or entertainment?

*Exactly what are you expected to talk about?* It isn't unheard of for a speaker unwittingly to deliver a presentation on the exact same subject this group heard at their luncheon meeting last month.

If necessary, negotiate to have your topic changed to a subject closer to what you already know a lot about. For example, if they want you to discuss the peculiarities of dog behavior, and you are experienced only with collies (or with cats), have the topic focused or changed.

(As we'll discuss in Chapter Five, the question to pose to yourself isn't "What should I talk about?" but "What do I *want* to talk about?")

*How much does the audience already know, believe or feel about your topic?* Most of us give presentations at work. We present an aspect of, problem with or solution to a business concern to associates who already know a great deal about our subject. If you deliver a paper at a conference, your colleagues may not know exactly what you're going to talk about but they know the field. The same is true when you deliver a report to a club or charitable organization. In situations where audience members are not your colleagues, your liason may be able to tell you how much they know. If she can't, ask her for a few phone numbers so you can do some quick interviews.

You do not want to tell people things they already know, ask them to do what they are already doing or to think about something they've struggled with for years. Nobody was ever insulted by a speaker who assumed too much about her audience's brains, open-mindedness or compassion. It is better to overestimate your audience than to infuriate them. Is there agreement among group members on the issues? Do not make assumptions about what people may believe. Ask your liaison.

*Are they looking forward to hearing you?* Is your audience being "strongly encouraged" (meaning "forced") to attend? (Is your talk a class or compulsory training workshop for them?)

*Will your audience eat or drink before your talk?* People who are half lit can't concentrate. After a heavy meal people feel sleepy. You might want to shorten your talk and be prepared to delete specific sections of it once underway. People who are on the way down from an alcoholic high tend to feel headachy and grouchy. Be brief and resolve not to take their irritation personally.

*Will people be drifting in and out while you talk?* If you aren't prepared for a casual coming and going and a bit of noise at the exits, you may become unduly nervous when people "walk out on you."

*Will they be in a rush to leave?* If you speak just before a lunch break when everyone is hungry or if you are the final speaker before the crowd rushes off to a gala party, you may want to keep it extra short. An audience in a giddy, anticipatory mood may not be very receptive, especially to a serious talk.

*What other speakers has this group heard recently?* How did they react to them? If Toni Morrison or Jay Leno or Jeanne Kilbourne appeared the week before, don't be heartbroken if you are a bit of a letdown by contrast; some speakers are very hard acts to follow. On the other hand, if the previous speaker put the group to sleep with a disappointing, overly technical address about the fish in Lake Michigan, you may seem dramatic and wonderful by comparison.

*Is this usually a responsive group?* How much do they ordinarily react? If you have been alerted ahead of time that the group is shy or apathetic, you can brace your psyche accordingly. We tend to overreact to what people "think" of us. Don't imagine you are a failure if the applause is only perfunctory or if you have to use every trick in Chapter Eight to get them to participate or to ask questions.

*What are the current "hot buttons"?* During conversation with your liaison, ask if there's anything (a tragedy, a howlingly funny incident) that has happened lately. You don't want inadvertently to trigger either embarrassment or hysteria with the wrong joke or anecdote. What's going on? What are the issues of the moment? What's the story with the group's politics? What is absorbing their interest and energy at the moment?

*What are the demographics?* What is the age range? What is the educational background of most of the audience? What is the economic status of the group? Will it be a racially mixed group? What will the male/female ratio be?

*What color is the backdrop?* Your lovely white suit will become invisible if the stage curtain is also white. Your nifty red dress will look tacky against a burgundy wall.

*What will the audience be wearing?* You might want to wear a Greek festival costume if you're speaking about ethnic dance.

You may want to select your outfit to "underwhelm" them if they're threatened by you. As a general rule, however, find out what the group will be wearing and then wear something yourself that is just a trifle dressier. The idea is to establish yourself as "The Speaker," to set yourself slightly apart from the crowd, to show them that you are taking their invitation seriously enough to dress up a little for them, and yet to look enough like them to establish yourself as a person with whom they can identify. For example, if you are going to talk to a high school class, the liaison (probably a teacher or student) will probably inform you that most of the audience will be in blue jeans. You may then elect to wear casual slacks and an ordinary (though not beat-up) sweater.

It's difficult enough to get through an audience's prejudices about your topic. Don't innocently dress in a way that will trigger their stereotypes about you. If your clothing style will seem unconventional to the group, you run the risk of siphoning off energy better spent on your topic itself. You may engender a new controversy by under- or overdressing according to their sartorial norms, when you want your topic to be the sole object of attention or controversy.

On the other hand, you may feel that it's a sellout to cave in to anyone's notions of how a "real" woman looks, how a "proper" business woman dresses. Sexy clothes—that is "sexy" as defined by *Cosmopolitan* magazine or *Playboy*—are always a bad idea. Both men and women find them distracting. Dark glasses (sunglasses) harm the two-way live current of person-to-people contact you need.

We are not suggesting that you change who you are, but rather that you ask your liaison to make you aware of the possible reactions of the group to your clothes so that you won't be floored. You may regard your outfit as a stage prop for your public self, a costume, strategically chosen to achieve the effect you want.

Now, before you sit down to write, make sure you have

cleared all of the arrangements with your liaison. Here is our checklist:

*How large is the group?*  Few things are more dreadful than preparing oneself for an armchair chat around a fireside only to find a crowd of five hundred gathered, or vice versa.

*What time are you supposed to begin speaking?*  Tell your liaison you want to arrive early to check the microphone, lights and general setting, so somebody will be there to meet you and unlock doors for you. What's the name of the person who will greet you?

*Will you be expected to spend informal time with the group?*  Do they want you to circulate and meet people? Will there be some sort of reception and/or do they want you to remain after your talk to chat with people informally? Do they expect you to do anything (pose for photographs, sign autographs, have a meal) prior to the speech? Who will sit next to you at dinner, on the dais?

*How long are you supposed to talk?*  How long do speakers usually talk to this group? Are you expected to entertain questions after your presentation? What is the usual ratio between prepared remarks and the questions-and-answer portion?

*Will you be "onstage" for a long time before you speak?*  Your decision about shoes, short versus long skirt or slacks may be influenced by whether you will be seated or standing while you are on view and by how long you will be "sized up" before you speak.

*What is the format?*  Inquire about the overall schedule for the day. Who will speak before you? After you? For how many minutes? Must you acknowledge anyone in your opening?

*Should you bring a guest?*   If this is an affair to which speakers are expected to bring a spouse, or Significant Other, where will she/he sit? On the dais with you? If your guest is a man, what are the men wearing? If the invitation to speak does not specify guests, ask if it would be all right to bring a friend anyway. You may want to invite somebody who will give you moral support and who can help you evaluate what went right/ wrong afterwards.

*If you are invited to solo, would they be willing to take two of you?*   A team talk is a great idea if you are nervous and would feel calmer sharing the chores. If the subject is controversial a second person might lend credibility to your viewpoint. Two personalities and styles might help offset the audience's tendency to stereotype a representative of your issue.

*Are the directions complete?*   This is vital. If you get the wrong room number in a huge school or office building you may waste precious time. How long does it take to get there? Should you allow extra time for the hour of the day? Will there be holiday traffic?

*How will you get to the talk?*   Are they going to send someone to pick you up? If you are to be met at the airport how will you recognize your driver and where will you meet?

*Where can you park?*   How much will it cost?

*Is there an honorarium? Ask about expenses.*   Will you be paid? How much? When? To whom do you want the check made out?

   If you plan to contribute the honorarium you have requested to a charity or to the organization you are representing, perhaps you would like your introducer to mention it. If there is a program printed for audience members, ask to have your contribution mentioned in it.

Will you be reimbursed for travel expenses (taxi, gas or mileage)? Do they want receipts? If you are speaking at no charge, perhaps it would be appropriate to set up "collection baskets" at the exits with a request for contributions for your expenses or for the organization on whose behalf you are speaking.

Do not sell yourself short. If the group usually pays for speakers, don't volunteer to speak for free or for any amount less than the fair market value established by the group. It is amazing how many people believe that women can afford to give away their time, talents and expertise—or that since a good speaker makes it *look* easy, putting together a talk is a snap. Note that precise financial arrangements should always be confirmed in writing.

*What publicity is being done?* Any advertising (in-house memo, flyers and posters, radio announcements and so on) should be cleared with you for content. If your liaison person is inexperienced, perhaps you could suggest publicity as a way of attracting an audience. Supply a photo and a sheet of biographical information or a sample flyer regarding you and your topic. (Also ask your liaison to clip and send you copies of flyers, newspaper articles and the like for your records.)

*Who will introduce you?* How and when will you have an opportunity to talk to that person (in person, on the phone or through letters) to give her suggestions? (See Chapter Nine.)

*In what arrangement will your audience be seated?* Request two things: the most intimate setting possible for the number of people you will be talking to (you look pathetic standing at a podium in front of a mike if there are only twelve people in the auditorium); and a way to refer to your notes that is convenient and does not seem pretentious in the setting.

Will you be on an auditorium stage, in an aromatic banquet hall full of folks chowing down or in a tiny conference room?

Do you want your audience to be seated in rows, in a circle or at tables?

Keep in mind that you want to be situated so that everyone can see and hear you. Depending on the size of the group, this may mean walking to the front, or standing (even though all the other speakers stayed seated) or being seated on a platform higher than the audience. If you can have the chairs arranged in a semicircle or a circle for a small group, or concentric circles for a larger group, you can achieve a warmer atmosphere than you can when nobody can see anyone else.

Ask for a straight-backed chair for yourself. You will feel more in command, sit up straighter and probably be at a higher level (so that you can be seen easily) than those who sink into soft and comfy armchairs.

*Will there be a podium?* Take nothing for granted. If you expect to speak at a lectern and your host expects you to rise and talk at your place, you may be unnerved. If you are particularly tall or short, ask how high the podium is or how high the table and table lectern, taken together, will reach. You may need to request different equipment if the group isn't going to be able to see your face over the rostrum. Senator Barbara Boxer (Dem. CA) often stands on a box, but she probably has a retinue to schlepp the box from hall to hall. Suggest a box of a specified height, width and strength to stand on, or ask if they can substitute a table with a table lectern. If you are going to be using an antique podium, carved of mahogany in the days when 5'4" was considered tall for a man, and you stand 5'10", request a substitute. You don't want to have to bow from the waist every time you refer to your cue cards.

Note that inexperienced liaisons don't think about things like "modesty panels" (tablecloths). Without them, your legs show whether you are seated or standing. This is important to consider for panel presentations when you are on view for a much longer time than your actual speaking turn. If your face registers serenity

*If you* must *sit on a sofa, don't melt into it.*

and your legs are twisted into Syrian cheese strings, you will give a double message to the audience. (You may also prefer trousers or a long skirt in these circumstances.)

Sometimes speakers' tables are very long, with a mike at each place. At other times participants have to share a mike, passing it back and forth to take turns speaking. Sometimes there is just one freestanding mike, and speakers must rise and walk to it in order to talk. Ask!

*If you have physical disabilities.* Even when your liaison

thinks she understands your situation, she probably doesn't. Spell out what you will need and how you plan to perform *in detail*. For example, do you want a chair, an assistant on the stage with you to re-ask questions louder and more clearly, someone to carry your oxygen? If an unsurmountable difficulty shows up that neither of you anticipated, carry on. Do not allow the audience to panic. You cope every day, after all; they can cope with whatever last-minute adaptation must be made.

*Will you be miked?* Your arrival time may depend on whether you want to do a mike check.

*Planning the question-and-answer session.* One of the most important ways in which a liaison person can help you is in arrangements for the question-and-answer part of your talk. She can solicit written but unsigned questions from audience members ahead of time and/or just before a break. She can promise to ask a question if hands don't shoot up immediately. She can "plant" another questioner in the audience if the group is unusually shy or unresponsive. (See the "Making Sure There Are Questions" section of Chapter Eight.)

*Arranging time signals.* Prearrange time signals with your liaison so you will know when your time is running out. Many speakers like to set up three signals: five minutes to go (hand up with five fingers spread wide); wrap it up, hurry (rolling arms in a football official's "illegal motion" signal); and time's up (forming a *T* with the hands).

The liaison can stand at the back of the room throughout your presentation to do this for you and also to signal you any time your voice drops so low that you become inaudible. If the liaison can't do this, ask her to make arrangements with someone else to coach you from the rear.

You still must use a watch with a large face, large numerals and hands, one that you can see without seeming to look at it. Arrangements for signaling can break down.

*Prearranging the use of visual aids or handouts.* If you plan to use a slide projector or other piece of equipment or hand out printed material, the arrangements must be absolutely clear. Do you want to pass out a graphic to everyone in the audience at a particular moment in your talk? Ask your liaison person to have "runners" ready to distribute handouts quickly and efficiently on a signal from you. Do you want someone to stand near the lights to avoid an awkward delay when it's time to show your slides? Ask!

*Request water.* Don't assume that everyone knows that a speaker appreciates having at least a cup of the stuff on hand. Ask for it.

*Could someone operate your tape recorder?* Could some kind soul tape your talk on the recorder you're bringing so you can hear it later?

*Where are you supposed to sit/go upon leaving the podium?* It will not do to stride purposefully into a broom closet.

In our experience, liaisons are often much more nervous than speakers. Don't let the liaison's nerves infect you! Reassure her by knowing just what you need and radiating confidence. Express your appreciation for her role as facilitator. Thank her on site, and afterward, in writing.

Develop a moderator's guide if you speak frequently. Remember, liaisons want your "backstage" requests and suggestions so they can help you to produce better results "onstage." Include your policy about audio- or videotaping your presentation. Is the press welcome to cover your talk? Do you need flipcharts, markers, an overhead projector, slide projector or film screen?

All of this probably seems like a lot of trouble. Actually, it takes longer to describe helpful logistics than to arrange them. Give yourself the best possible chance for success by making sure that nothing will distract from your fabulous speech. For how to write that fabulous speech, read on.

# CHAPTER FIVE

# Writing to Be Heard

*"No one will ever know the pains I have taken to achieve so little."*
—Claude Monet

Writing a talk, even a very short one, is hard work, particularly if you haven't tried it before. In addition to the difficulties most of us have writing anything, there are specific problems with speech writing. Unlike literature, oral style is not for beauty or permanence. The effect of the moment is what counts. Writing to be heard is different from writing to be read. A great presentation may read badly and a bad presentation read wonderfully.

## Why Is Speech Writing Different?

When people read, they reread. Watch someone read a newspaper article, and you will notice that her eyes drift back up from time to time to reread sentences or whole paragraphs. She would not have this advantage if she were listening. When we listen, rhetorical devices such as repetition compensate for the fact that we cannot reread significant passages. (Repetition also impacts the drama of a speech, heightening our emotional reaction.) Our difficulty hearing and remembering (as opposed to reading and rereading) is also the reason long complex sentences are usually inappropriate. Technical information, especially numbers, should be carefully spaced and repeated. Foreign phrases, unusual or unfamiliar titles and so forth should be clearly enunciated, spoken slowly and if necessary explained.

You use punctuation when you write (italics, bold type, capital letters) to let the reader know what is important, what she should pause to think over before reading on. When you walk you must use inflection, pauses and pacing to make your points.

In short, oral language requires more repetition and simpler sentence structure than written language. Short, terse sentences may bother a reader, but not a listener.

Preparation for a speech is at least 50 percent rehearsal. You are both playwright and the cast—don't neglect the second phase by getting a late start with the first.


## Begin at Once: "Give It Ten"

As soon as you agree to give a talk, retire to your office, put up a "go away" sign on your cubicle or hide in the women's room in order to take speech coach Judith O'Rourke's excellent advice: "Give it ten." Begin to jot down ideas. Keep writing for ten uninterrupted minutes of your fullest concentration. Blank paper is terrifying. The longer you wait, the more difficult writing becomes, and almost any beginning is better than none. If you accept the invitation to speak while you're caught away from your home turf, start making notes on tissue, napkins, tatty pieces of paper or in the notebook you carry. If you panic and speech ideas don't come, then start by writing "The purpose of this speech is . . ." or "I think I will write about. . . ," "In general, I will discuss. . . ," "I especially want to emphasize . . ." until you are ready to start thinking about communicating to those people to whom you have just agreed to talk. The ten minutes you invest immediately will create valuable momentum and shift your entire psychology from anxiety and procrastination to finishing something you've already got under control.

## Feel Communicative

As you begin, think about your audience. Intensify your interest and impulse to communicate. Write *to* them, remembering that "they" are not a monolith. An audience is one person, then another, then another. We *talk* with one another. Try to feel this way as you begin your first draft. Remembering that an audience is not an "it" will help you to establish a tone for your speech—light or serious, warm or intense or sincere or funny. How can you best convey your message to *them*?

Try rereading some of your old speeches, or John Bartlett's *Familiar Quotations,* to put yourself in a speech-writing frame of mind. The most important step may be putting yourself into the proper spirit. If necessary, imagine that someone *else* is giving your speech. What would her objectives be?

## Writing the First Draft

About 80 percent of what your presentation will eventually include should come off the top of your head in the first draft. Keeping your audience in mind, begin to rough out ideas. What is your point? Write down, in stream-of-consciousness style, everything you think you might want to say. Don't dismiss any ideas; you can edit later. Don't worry about grammar or spelling or scintillating language or organization or being perfect or even being good. Just get thoughts on paper. Write until you've worn out your information supply. It is easier to edit a mishmash of material than to create from scratch. That's why there are more good editors than good writers. Just get something in front of you—everything will be easier from then on.

When your first draft notes are finished you are ready to fill in the gaps with research. Research does not mean learning a whole subject area and then trying to write a speech about it. When we say "research" we mean checking quotations or statistics for accuracy, or reading the newest material on your topic to make sure your information is current, or rereading source material to refresh your memory.

As a general guideline, refuse a speaking engagement if you must spend more than 20 percent of your preparation time on research. If you aren't utterly familiar with your subject, you'll feel like a fraud and your self-confidence will be undermined. Most of your preparation time should be divided between editing and rehearsing.

*Don't overburden your memory; carry a notebook.* At every stage of speech writing and editing, ideas, turns of phrase and lines of reasoning will occur to you, often at odd times. Relaxed moments when you seem to be doing nothing (riding an elevator, waiting in a line) are often times of high creativity. Your subconscious is full of good information that likes to escape when you are lost in thought staring into the refrigerator. Jot down your ideas and save them. If you love your topic, you will dash off a great many more quips and quotes than you will be able to use . . . for *this* speech. If your subject bores you (and many work-related presentations may), it is even more important to let your imagination loose. A fresh approach to dull material will often occur to you only when you are doing something mundane like brushing your hair and feel free from the constraints of an official writing session.

Writers, filmmakers and strategists in business and politics often share a nocturnal quirk: they *use* the moments between sleeping and waking because these are unusually productive times for the imagination. Instead of getting a good idea, rolling over to snooze and forgetting the idea by the next day, keep a pencil and notebook by your bed. You may have to scrawl in the dark, but you won't lose the idea. You also may develop insomnia, but only for the duration.

Once you have finished your first draft and moved on to the research stage, abandon the writing for as long as you dare—a couple of days if you have a week to write it, a week if you have a month. You may not think about the talk in your conscious mind very often, but your subconscious will take over for you. Speech writing is like any other kind of writing; it benefits from latent periods, from lying fallow for a stretch of time. After a "fermenting" period you can return to your notes with a fresh perspective—with new phrases, notes you've been compiling, research you have completed. Because your subconscious mind has been composing the speech all along, you will have a much clearer understanding of what you want to say and your second draft will seem almost effortless.

## Editing Your First Draft for Organization

Much editing consists of reorganizing ideas into a different order. Reread your first draft and see if you know what your point is. This sounds like we are being funny but the major cause of confused disjointed unclear speech writing is confused disjointed unclear thinking. The reason most first drafts are such a mess is that the writer really doesn't know what she thinks and why until after she has tried out what she has written. The process of trying to make our thoughts clear on paper sometimes helps us see that they aren't such hot thoughts in the first place.

*Will it pass the paraphrase test?* The rule is to make positively, unequivocally certain that you have a point and that you state it so clearly that every person leaving the hall will be able to give a concise, coherent synopsis of your presentation. "Uh, she talked about baseball" is not good enough.

Several generations ago, orations lasting all day were commonplace. Today, a twenty-minute keynote is the norm. So don't be too ambitious. In a five-minute talk you can make one major point; in a twenty-minute talk you can probably support two. The most common, and fatal, speech writing mistake is trying to say too much. It is better to have one theme, stated powerfully and memorably, than to ramble around six points. Be strict with yourself when you make the final decision about what you plan to cover. We recognize that it is difficult to do this, especially if you know a great deal about your topic. Simplifying in many cases seems like falsifying. Alas, you must make choices. (It helps to remember that if you put in too much your audience won't remember it anyway.)

Here's an example from a Levi Strauss & Co. workshop participant:

*Before:*
My manager and I had limited contact because he traveled a significant amount. He told me that he had certain perceptions of me and they caused him concern. Basically, he thought he had made a mistake in asking me to head the department and thought I would never be a success there. We discussed his perceptions and he agreed that I deserved an opportunity to prove them wrong. My next six months of assignments were specifically designed in order to provide evidence—whether positive or negative—to test his perceptions. My department consisted of myself, and eight others. The perception of the department was that it did enough to get by, but never did top quality work.

*Feedback:*
This will not pass the paraphrase test. Cut to the chase. Focus narrowly. Get rid of clutter. What is the main point?

*After:*
One year ago I was made head of a department. It was my last chance to stay with the company. My manager told me he thought he had made a mistake in hiring me. The staff I was to manage were perceived as losers.

We didn't need to know that her manager traveled a lot and his absences contributed to his misperceptions.

Here are the two steps to rewriting your first draft:

1. *Make an outline.* Outline that jumbled first draft as if you were taking notes from a stranger's speech. Pick out the major points and subsidiary points of what this person is trying to say. Now rearrange the outline so it is clear and easy to follow.

2. *Write a new speech from the outline.* Use as much of the old stuff as is salvageable. (These steps take a long time if you are new at speech writing, so start early).

Certain topics lend themselves logically to chronological or sequential organization (organizing a conference, how to repair a carburetor, the story of your life). This is fine as long as you are careful to vary your language and rhythm and not give a speech on the Legislative History of the Equal Rights Amendment that goes like this. "In 1970 women gathered . . . , in 1971 there were some changes . . . , in 1972 Congress. . . ." Also avoid saying, "First, you take your complaint form to the Equal Employment Opportunity Commission . . . second, you attempt to conciliate the charge with your employer . . . third, you obtain a 'right to sue' letter . . . fourth. . . ." These kinds of transitions are too repetitious.

## Write the Second and Subsequent Drafts Out Loud

Editing a speech differs from editing material intended to be read because you want to know not only if it is well organized and clear but also how it sounds. The best way to find out is to write the second (and each subsequent) draft out loud. This isn't about reading; it is about talking. You don't want to talk like you write, you want to write like you talk. So say it. Write out loud. Is it easy to say? Do you come alive when you say it? Does it have variety? Do you sound warm and friendly or cold and flat? Do you like that woman you hear talking?

## Editing for Style

There are three main points to remember when you edit for style:

1. There is *no* subject that cannot be made interesting.

2. This is a speech, not an essay. Write something you can *feel* while you say it.

3. This is a conversation, even though only one person is talking. You want to sound like yourself, not a fax or a book.

If you write an article or a memo (instead of a talk) you get stuck delivering your article or essay out loud to the group. If you want the talk to have a conversational, sharing, making-friends tone, you will have to write it in. If you want people to feel talked with (not *at*) you will have to write it that way. A one-to-one quality cannot come from your delivery alone.

The following suggestions will help you avoid a grim, turgid talk:

*Don't say the title.*   Speech titles or topics are for publicity, for the printed program or for the introducer to announce.

*Skip the fillers.*   Greetings such as "Good afternoon, ladies and gentlemen" aren't necessary. Jump right in with your first line.

"Thank you" is too often a filler. If you have some reason to say it (a nice introduction merits a turn of the head and thank you to the introducer, or a round of applause requires a thanks to the group), go ahead.

*Toss out your first paragraph.* Most of the pomposity, arch jokes and phony "attention getters" are probably in your first paragraph. See if you can throw away the introductory paragraph and start with the sentences that sound involved, invested, excited and emotionally "there." You want to begin naturally and as if you were talking among friends.

*Avoid generalizations.* The more you generalize the more you are likely to say something that is not true or offensive. Don't say "women think" if you mean "the African-American women at Smith in 1994 indicated on a survey. . . ." The more specific you are the less likely you are to be wrong.

*Repeat references.* If a listener tunes out briefly, don't punish her by forcing her to wonder who "he" is for the next thirty minutes. Don't overuse "he," "she," "it," "they," "that" or "those." Repeat "Jeffrey" and "bowling ball."

*Don't make lists.* The following is an example of list-making that may be fine for an article, but will *not* work in a speech:

> If you want to know how to start a refuge for battered wives . . . my advice is to start at the local level: form coalitions and task forces; research applicable state laws and city ordinances; investigate policies and procedures for law enforcement (police, district attorney, and the courts); gather statistics from every conceivable source; canvass emergency housing and note admission policies; determine what services are already available and which need to be established; draw up proposals based on that information; make funding agencies aware of the need; lobby for remedial legislation at every level of government; demand a reordering of priorities in government and foundation spending; and don't stop until all necessary programs are realized.[7]

There is absolutely no way you could deliver those excellent ideas orally without sounding as though you were reading a shopping list. Your voice will get sing-songy and monotonous.

Sequential ideas which work well in written text will have to be rewritten for a speech to eliminate the sameness that is bound to creep into the delivery.

*Use concrete examples.* If you want to talk about day care, tell a story about one family that illustrates your point. If you want to discuss hunger in the United States, use a composite person to illustrate your facts. (For example, "George Carver lives in Appalachia. He is six years old. George eats chalk, paste and grass. He can't pay attention in school because he's starving. . . .") Your audience will respond more attentively to a case history than they can to the information that many people in this country are undernourished.

If you talk about drought conditions in Africa, make your facts come alive by telling how drought affects one tribe. If you are explaining urban transportation, tell an anecdote about one person who can't get from her home to her job. Audiences have a hard time getting charged up over an abstract concept or a rhetorical generalization.

*Use active voice.* Passive constructions delete responsibility, which is why business correspondence is rife with them. Passive voice eliminates agency and accountability. Your speech goes flat, however, if the action is happening *to* someone or something. It is hard to visualize the scene if you have eliminated the actors. In the following paragraph, the parenthetical comments indicate how the passive voice steals impact from a speech.

> Dear Mr. Rector, After a careful review of the information (*By whom? Who reviewed?*) provided, (*By whom? Clinton didn't review the information submitted by Mr. Rector's lawyer.*) your request for executive clemency has been denied. (*Meaning: "I have decided to order your execution."*) Sincerely, Bill Clinton

Make the subject of each sentence act.

| Passive Voice (Wrong) | Active Voice (Correct) |
|---|---|
| It has occurred to me. It seems to me. | I think, I believe. |
| The bomb is dropped by the airplane. | The pilot bombed the village and killed the people. |
| It is thought. | The board said. |
| Women were denied equal pay. | The vice president of personnel denied equal pay to women. |
| The problem is to be investigated. | Our committee will investigate. |

*Check your verbs for color.* Read through the whole speech and replace every dull verb with one that expresses the precise shade of action you want to convey. Use a thesaurus or dictionary. For instance, why say "I walked in" if you really strolled, wandered, dashed or lurched? Beware of the verbs to have, to be and got. If you *have* a cold, a drink or a hard time, you aren't *sick* with a cold, *gulping* a drink or *struggling*. If you pick the right verb you don't need four adverbs.

*Use visual language.* Help the audience make movies in their heads while you talk. Once they've seen you, they've seen you. It doesn't take long to exhaust the entertainment potential of trying to decide if you're wearing real pearls or fake ones. From then on, the group members need to be able to visualize what you're talking about, to run a mental video. Here's an example from another student:

*Before:*
    Immediately, I ran into resistance from my students. I heard that I was only a social worker, that I was too inex-

perienced to know what I was talking about, that I was too young, and, of course, that I was a woman. Any of these all too frequent remarks and innuendos could have gotten the best of me. Instead, each seemed to strengthen my determination to myself, to the teaching profession, and to women, that I had something of value to contribute.

*Feedback:*
Conceptual, general, abstract. The audience can't "see" it. Make a movie instead.

*After:*
I was so worn down by then, I stood on the library steps nearly in tears. Somehow I kept talking. I said, "John, you don't have to believe in me. Believe in the dean who appointed me and be in class tomorrow. Period."

I was angry with myself for shaking in front of him. But John was there the next day. A week later, he stopped by my desk. With real respect, he asked, "How am I doing, Ms. Ellison?"

Use examples, quotes and anecdotes, instead of describing a situation generally or abstractly. One vignette or picture in the minds of listeners is worth pages of narrative.

| **Dull** | **Better** |
|---|---|
| Students pay a yearly athletic fee. | Students pull the athletic fee from their jeans each year. |

*Avoid extended metaphors.* Comparisons are great, but please, no "ship of state foundering on the rocks of insolvency after a rough sea of fiscal irresponsibility crying for a new captain with a fresh economic mandate as the lighthouse to guide us into a harbor. . . ." The longer you stretch a comparison, the harder it becomes to make two ideas or objects match up. Maybe you can prove that a girl is like a rose in a hundred ways—but why bother?

## Using Statistics

Numbers require a bit more concentration from your listeners so follow these tips to make it easier for your audience.

*Space them.* Percentages, dollars and years are all numbers, which a reader sorts out easily. Listeners cannot absorb more than two or three numbers at a time. Spread out numerical information and pad it with English.

*Repeat them.* It's harder to remember numbers than words. Radio announcers repeat the phone number for call-ins dozens of times in an hour. Repeat key statistics.

*Make them visual.* Even when you are reading them, large numbers are meaningless until you stop to think about them, to visualize what they connote. A group can grasp the visual significance of a football field better than they can the concept of one hundred yards. If you explain that something is the size of a cockroach, your image will have more impact than a measurement in centimeters. Don't just tell your audience how many feet tall something is, compare it in size to an object they are familiar with—a well-known skyscraper, a telephone booth or your podium.

| **Dull** | **Better** |
|---|---|
| Americans spend an average of thirteen hours per year on civic or community improvements. | The average American spends more time each year putting on underarm deodorant than contributing to their community. |
| According to a 1992 study funded by the National Institute of Drug Abuse, 13 percent of adult American women have been raped at least once, 75 percent by | According to a 1992 study funded by the National Institute of Drug Abuse, one in eight American women have been raped. Statistically, that means at least |

| Dull | Better |
|---|---|
| someone they knew. | twenty-one women sitting in this room right now have been raped. |
| We do have the funds to establish a new language lab. But the school committee has different priorities. | A new language lab would cost on a yearly basis what the athletic department spends in two months. |

Give the actual numbers when your talk demands precision and accuracy. You may use a comparison afterward.

*Suit statistics to the audience.* To a group of Girl Scouts: "That means that the protein in a single hot dog is more than some kids eat in a whole week." To a group of successful business people: "The cost of one drink before lunch would supply milk for ten children for a week."

## Jargon

Rehearse your speech with other people. You will be able to judge by their facial expressions whether the speech contains technical language or a special word that should be defined or deleted. Even when you're talking to your own colleagues, whom you know understand your jargon, it's refreshing and often enlightening to try to speak English.

## Clichés

If it sounds like something you've heard a hundred times, don't say it. We already know that kites are high, foxes are sly and mules are stubborn. Rephrase anything that sounds hackneyed. (See the section on using clichés in Chapter Two.)

## Violent Metaphors

Find nonviolent substitutes for belligerent words and phrases such as *enemy, destroy, attack, go ballistic, shoot down an idea, nuke, let them have it with both barrels.* Win/lose language may compromise your own attitude—of community and of partnering—which is essential to successful negotiation and persuasion. An alternative to "shoot from the hip," for example might be "respond impulsively." An alternative to "bring in the heavy artillery" might be "use powerful arguments." A "straight shooter" is someone who tells the truth.

## Can You Say It?

Will the audience have forgotten the beginning of your sentence by the time you wind your way through all the commas and clauses and arrive at the end? Can you say the thought (whether a phrase or a sentence) in one breath? Don't distort the sense of your phrases by having to pause for breath in the wrong places. Shorten your sentences if your delivery sounds choppy or uneven. Avoid alliteration (Peter Piper picked a peck of pickled peppers). Avoid phrases that might turn into something embarrassing if misspoken (seven sheet slitters slitting sheets). The only way to tell if this will happen is to *write and rehearse out loud.*

Double-check to make certain any difficult concept or central argument is repeated often enough. Make it clear when you move from one point to the next. Be sure, if you have promised three main points, to deliver three.

Speech is *talk,* so say "she's, they're, don't, can't." "She is, they are, do not, cannot'' sound too formal unless you are pronouncing the words in full for emphasis.


## Quotations

Audiences love quotes, but you undercut their effectiveness if you present them clumsily. Avoid saying ''quote . . . unquote.'' Instead, use inflection to indicate that you are quoting and introduce the quotation in one of the ways shown here:

> ''. . . ,'' said Polly Grant, ''is. . . .''
> Barbara Anthony expressed her advice on . . . in this way: ''. . .''
> Alan Hewat has said, ''. . .''
> ''. . .'' (using strong inflection). In those words, Houston attorney Janna Ivey expressed. . . .

Sometimes you don't want to quote someone directly, but you wish to acknowledge that the ideas you are expressing are not original. Try: ''In considering . . . , I've been greatly helped by Artemis March's brilliant theoretical analysis.'' Or, ''Obviously, these notions have been influenced by Ralph Nader's work, especially *Unsafe at Any Speed.*''

Don't say: ''People seem to feel. . . .'' Say, ''One remark I overheard is typical. She said, ''. . . .''

Avoid lengthy quotations; the audience came to hear you. Also, don't quote the same source over and over again. If your topic is sex, don't just stick to Masters and Johnson. Your four-year-old, Mae West and *Our Bodies, Ourselves* have had things to say, too.


## Writing to Persuade

As you are writing your talk, try to assess what will touch the personal welfare of the individuals you will address. Determine your overall approach according to their preconceived notions about your topic. Most groups, of course, are neutral or generally sympathetic.

*Hostile groups.* If the information you have gleaned from your liaison indicates that the audience may be hostile to you personally, hostile to the measures you advocate or hostile to the group you represent, your talk must emphasize beliefs and experiences you have in common with that audience. Otherwise the group will not believe you understand or care about their concerns and will disregard what you say.

Honor the opinions of others by taking them into consideration when you compose your talk. Acknowledge by statement or clear implication the significant opinions of your audience. Start positively; concede points to the opposition if you can. Where is the common ground? To avoid going on the defensive, you must be ready for anything, but don't burden yourself with a big chip on your shoulder. If you cannot bring yourself to care about the fears, needs and concerns of a group don't go talk to them. *You* are hostile to *them.*

*Apathetic audiences.* If you anticipate that the members of the group will be tired or uncomfortable or that they didn't want to come to hear you in the first place or could care less about your subject, then you must write a talk that will surprise them out of their lethargy or irritation. Startling statements and vivid illustrations are especially important if the group is bored. To intensify interest in you and your topic, present your information in as novel a way as you can. Look for fresh angles, words and examples that will jar them out of their complacency. You may have to lead off with your strongest material. Arousing curiosity, using humor, accenting the unusual and creating mystery are your antidotes to their ennui. Drama is important for apathetic groups, but remember that a hostile group calls for calm evidence and reasoning.

Remember, we are not recommending that you become a

chameleon. Your ideas, values and experience are unique and important. Obtaining information ahead of time helps you feel psychologically prepared and may help you express your ideas, but it isn't going to cause you to change, and it shouldn't. If it helps you understand and have compassion for a group to consider what they want, believe and care about, then you will be more persuasive. If you are trying to adopt an entirely new persona, or sugarcoat your unpopular convictions, you'll feel phony and it won't work.

Here are the steps to *persuasion organization,* or how to make a mad idea seem plausible:

1. Open by securing the attention of your audience. Rivet them with a ringing phrase.

2. State the problem. Color it with an anecdote or a quotation.

3. Prove the existence of the problem. Use statistics, quotations and examples.

4. Describe the unfortunate consequences of the problem or prevailing conditions. How do these consequences affect this audience? Persuade them to be concerned. Make them feel personally dissatisfied with the way things are.

5. Is there a solution? What changes does the audience fear or desire?

6. State your solution. Document why it is the most effective solution.

7. Show how your solution will benefit the audience and paint a glowing picture of how life will be once your idea has been enacted. "Sales, particularly in the south and southwest, should increase 15 percent in the first six months." Stress the advantages for this audience of the changes you suggest, and quantify those benefits if you can (money to be saved, percentage of time faster, number of staff hours saved).

8. Anticipate and have answers ready for the objections you know are coming.

9. Invite action. This is the climax of your speech. Appeal to your audience's motives (pleasure? advancement? sympathy? pride? loyalty?).

The tone of your speech may be angry, hopeful, conciliatory or all three. The following three pointers can make your speech even more effective.

*Create dissatisfaction.* Point out the problems with the way things are, or make your audience aware of the dissatisfaction that is lurking under the surface.

*Give them a halo.* You best persuade an audience if you can convince them that they figured out the solution by themselves, and the change you advocate is merely the next step on the continuum of their already good decisions and excellent behavior. Consultant Jayne Townsend calls it "giving them a halo and then making them wear it."

*Get on strong and get off strong.* Pay particular attention to your opening remarks and your conclusion. They may be all the audience remembers. A strong ringing ending, "Give me liberty or give me death," is not the only way to be memorable. The final sentence can be delivered with quiet sincerity yet leave the listeners at an emotional high point.

## Pitching an Idea, Proposal or Project at Work: Influencing the Decision Environment

Most decisions are made *before* the so-called decision meeting. Most people will take a position long before the meeting starts. We must not cling to the fantasy that if our wording is eloquent and our convictions are solid, that the strength of our arguments will carry the day. Clear arguments and a strong, persuasive presentation do help. But they are usually too late. If you haven't done your homework backstage, your eloquence on stage may be wasted. Having leverage requires confronting people's doubts about your proposal at *every* stage of the decision-making process.

*Identify objections.* How can you scratch them if you don't know where they itch? Focus squarely on the points of resistance to the project. What feelings, needs, wants and concerns do those resisters have? How do they see things? The approach, the style you want to establish is a sincere and honest interest in helping meet their needs. If, from the beginning, you concentrate on the ways *they'll* win, how they'll benefit, you'll create a "you-centered" proposition that will be difficult for resisters to object to.

Casually interview people. "What do you like most about it? What do you want to change?"

> "Josh, I'm going to propose X. How do you feel about it? How do you think Rosemary will feel about it?"
>
> "Charles, you seem to know Rosemary Malone quite well, and work with her successfully. I'm going to propose X. Do you have any insights or advice?"

Your intelligence gathering will enable you to tackle objections and concerns head on, rather than wait for them to surface in the question-and-answer session.

*Lobby for your idea in advance.* Pre-sell components of your recommendation or your proposal through casual conversations. Get people enthusiastic about bits and pieces. See if you can reach not just the nominal leaders, but the people who influence them. Ask other people to talk up your project. ("Gretchen is coming to you with a good idea. I hope you'll give her a careful hearing.'') Collect your IOUs. Ask for whatever help you need from those for whom you've done favors in the past.

*Use a team approach.* Whenever possible get help when persuading. Divide up the pre-meeting idea-marketing chores according to who has access, then divide up the presentation itself according to who has credibility or who relates well to key members of the group. Make sure the team does a run-through before the meeting. As consultant Jayne Townsend reminds us, "You aren't a team player if you won't let other people help you."

If your group leader has the nasty habit of blasting proposals before they've been fully articulated, a team approach and pre-selling will limit his or her autocratic ways. When four people at the table are invested in the success of the presentation, and a handful of others have heard enough before the meeting to want to hear more, the idea can't be dismissed quite so high-handedly or casually.

Finally, get a firm commitment to enough time and an advantageous time slot on the agenda (after the latecomers have snuck in, and before the early leavers sneak out).

## Your Mental Framework When Talking to Hostile Groups

You must keep the opposition's feelings, needs and wants foremost in your planning and your speech writing in order to make a you-centered proposition. You want to be able to say: "Here is how we can meet your goal. Here is how my proposal will bring you closer to your objectives."

Inspire your listeners to cooperation by giving them a good reputation to live up to. Honest, constant, highly specific appreciation raises standards. If frequent, highly specific appreciation motivates the people you supervise, why wouldn't it motivate decision-making groups? "What I especially liked was X. You can be especially proud of Y."

Decompress the group's anxiety by *starting with* their biggest worry or criticism. Surprise the opposition by addressing their most pressing objection first. Now you have their attention and respect. Although you negotiate the biggest sticking points last, address them first, so the group will be able to focus on the balance of your information and the discussion. Otherwise, they may assume the facts you present aren't relevant because of the sticking point. Plus, you won't be on the defensive when the criticisms and "buts" start.

> "It's going to cost two million more than we'd hoped. We intend to demonstrate that the savings, projected five years out, justify every penny."

Present your case. Because data. Because facts. Because figures. Express everything in terms of you-benefits. You have done your homework, so what you are asking for and the way you are presenting it is focused on measurable results for *them,* the very best for them.

Unfortunately, you must assume they haven't read whatever it is they were supposed to have read before the meeting. Instead of judging them for their laxity, automatically plan to recap the topic's importance to them, and how it is consistent with the organization's mission.

Ask for everything you want. You violate the spirit of negotiation and compromise by asking for less.


## After the Presentation

Your job doesn't end when your speech does.

*Pin down stalls and objections:*

"I hear you saying that if we can meet that condition, you are prepared to support the project."

"If I satisfy your need for more information, then do we have a deal?"

"If I satisfy your need for a lower cost, then do we have an agreement?"

"The training workshop budget I've presented is $19,000. If I can get the costs down to $15,000, do I have the green light to proceed?"

Agreement in principle isn't enough. You must get commitment to the next step. Pin 'em down.

"Should I schedule the workshop for October or November?"

"Do you agree? May I go forward? Do we have a deal? Do you want it in blue, green or yellow?"

"Rosemary, you've agreed it makes sense to begin Phase One immediately. Shall we meet on Monday at nine A.M.?"

*Follow up the meeting with a memo.*   Circulate immediately a memo reiterating all parties' decisions, agreements and commitments. ("Charles will have the graphics done by a week from Thursday.") Your memo should include honest, highly specific appreciation.

Compare your usual approach to the framework for persuasion we've just outlined. Is there anything you want to do differently from now on to exert more influence on decisions?

It is pure pleasure to say "yes" to some people—to give them what they want, to agree to what they ask, to let ourselves be persuaded by them. We say "yes" so readily because they care about us. They care how we (and the things we worry about) will be affected. We're inclined to say "yes" because they seem to appreciate not only our circumstances, but us. Nobody likes the smell of insincerity or manipulation. Nobody likes to feel "handled" or on the receiving end of a strategy or a technique. The formula we recommend will work (preselling, surrogate lobbying), but only if you mean it when you say, "I want to see us make the best decision, even if it isn't my recommendation."


## Is It YOU?

*"Be what you is."*
—Clifton Chenier

Does the speech sound like something you would say on a good day? Can you carry it off or is there something in it that might trip you up or embarrass you? Delete anything that doesn't feel "right." An elegant passage that would earn high marks in the *Times* literary supplement may *sound* ridiculous. If you have found a poem that states exactly what you want to convey, think twice before you use it. If you are not an actor, if you have never tried to recite poetry before, if you feel uncomfortable saying the words (much as you love to read them silently to yourself), skip it. This is also true of slang, even mild obscenity, descriptions of bodily functions, sexual allusions and many "jokes." If you can't carry it off, leave it out.


## Suggestions for Common Short Speeches

*Announcements.* The worst time to make an announcement is just as everyone is leaving the room; their belongings are gathered up, and the noise level is starting to rise. If you want people to make note of a time or date, you will have to announce it when they have their pencils handy. Clear the announcement with the person in charge of the meeting and ask for a specific place on the agenda or a specific time when you can make it. If the meeting is very informal, select a time to jump up when everyone will be willing to hear you.

Your whole voice has to say, "This is interesting." Most

announcers take the tone of "I'm saying this because I'm supposed to."

*Presenting a gift or award.*   A gift is usually a symbol of something significant. Stress the reason for giving rather than the gift itself. Don't praise the recipient too lavishly because it will embarrass everyone. Take your mind completely off yourself and put it on the recipient; it is her moment of glory. This is not your show in any way; do not direct attention to yourself. Be careful to hold the gift close to your body until you mean to hand it over. It is very awkward for the recipient if she holds out her hands expecting to take it and you pull it back.

If the occasion is a retirement, remember that this might be a difficult day for the retiree. Make your tribute warm; interview her past and current colleagues until you have a handle on the specifics of Ms. Senior's contribution and specifically why she'll be missed.

*Travel talks.*   Travel talks are almost always a pain to listen to. The speaker piles details on detail, and chooses the most beautiful adjectives and adverbs to describe what she saw. The problem is too much description and not enough about what happened or how the speaker responded to what she saw. (Also, have you ever noticed that nobody ever says anything *bad* about the scenery?)

Travel speeches lack animation and warmth because the travelers get written out of it. Yes, you want to describe what you saw, but please tell us about you, too.

For example: "We saw many children in Mexico—they were everywhere." So what? Did their industry or lovely manners make you feel guilty about your own? Did anything happen? How did it make you feel?

"The scenery was awesome." Who was awed? Were you?

*Acceptance speeches.*   An audience will forgive you anything if you are sincere. Be simple and brief. If you have received help from others, share the glory with them by emphasizing their role; a solo bow without the cast isn't fair.

Do not look at the prize, look at the person who is presenting it. Don't hold out your hands to take it until it is actually offered to you. As you say your thanks, turn to the audience. Hold the gift in a way that allows everyone else to see it, too. Don't drop the arm holding it to your side.

## Save Everything

Keep all your texts and outlines, both hard copy and on a computer disk. It is even a good idea to keep your experimental drafts, research cards, lists of phrases and alternative ways of stating the same idea or fact. Cannibalizing this collection of old material helps you prepare more efficiently for each talk. It gets you off the starting block faster and with less writer's anxiety, and reminds you what works and what doesn't for you. If you are asked to address the same group sometime down the road, a copy of your last talk to them will spare you needless redundancy. (New speakers assume it isn't humanly possible to forget a single second of that peak experience, but you will, you will.)

## Get Help

Speech writing should be a team sport. Ask other people to be your audio editors. After a certain point your objectivity is shot and you can't fix your speech yourself.

Now the arrangements and the writing are over. You have a more or less final draft of the content of your speech. Have you done what you set out to do? Do you like it? Good. It is time to format the zippy talk you've prepared into final delivery notes, then rehearse it and deliver it.

There is a story about President Woodrow Wilson that may comfort you at this point. When he was asked how long he would prepare for a ten-minute talk, he answered, "Two weeks." For a one-hour speech? "One week." For a two-hour speech? "I'm ready now."

A "professional" speaker, a heavyweight on the lecture circuit, demands complete information on what to expect. You don't want any surprises. Be gently fanatic about all the details with your liaison, and remember that "spontaneity" requires effort. Give yourself all the breaks you can—plenty of time, ample editing, clear notes and stand-up, out-loud rehearsals. Remind yourself that you don't want to be standing eyeball to eyeball with an audience thinking, "Oh, I wish I had taken the time to do it right."

# CHAPTER SIX

# Your Props: Notes and Visual Aids

The rehearsal stage begins when you are satisfied with both the content of your talk and the format of your notes. You will put yourself at a great practical advantage, as well as a psychological one, if you deliver your presentation from legible text that won't trip you up and that looks like it belongs to somebody who knows what she is doing. Sloppy notes can make you feel unprepared and disheveled, or even embarrassed and uneasy if others see them.

## Notes That Work

Computer users have to make two basic decisions about notes: Should I present the speech from the full-text or from an outline? Do I want my text on large index cards or on paper? Those who prefer to or must write and deliver talks from longhand notes have additional considerations.

*Print out notes.* Printing by hand is better than keyboarding short presentations because the act of printing is a memory aid. One generally remembers little of a text one copytypes.

*Never use real shorthand.* Shorthand is like a foreign language. Even if you have been using it for years, it requires translation in your head before you can speak the words out loud. Shorthand may confuse you in a tense moment.

*Abbreviating handwritten notes.* If you are completely comfortable with your own idiosyncratic abbreviations, you can abbreviate more and more over time for speech delivery. If you have ever gone blank, don't abbreviate! Write out any word you might forget under pressure.

Common abbreviations and symbols include:

∴  Therefore
2  Two, too or to
g  Any "ing" ending (walkg 2 the store)

Eventually you can begin to delete articles (the, an, a) and most vowels and word endings. For example:

*Full-text:*
"In glancing through back issues of *Sojourner* before coming to speak with you this evening, I noticed that there is a disproportionate number of complaints and suits based on sex discrimination filed in the state of Florida. I wondered if I had been invited to the land of sunshine or a lion's den."

*Abbreviated text:*
"In glancg thru back iss of *Soj* B4 comg 2 speak w/u this eve, I notcd there's a disprop # of C & S based on S. D.

fild in state Fla. I wonderd if I had bn invitd 2 land of sunshn or a lion's den.''

Once again, let us emphasize that you do not do this until you are sure you can. If you have any doubts, don't.

---

IN GLANCG THRU BACK ISS OF SOJ

B4 COMG 2 SPEAK W/U THIS EVE , I ⬇

NOTCD THERE'S A DISPROP # OF C&S

BASD ON S.D. FILD IN STATE FLA. I

WONDRD IF I HAD BN INVITD 2 LAND

OF SUNSHN OR A LION'S DEN.

O     1     O

---

IT IS THIS TREAT-

MENT — LIKE CHILDREN OR

ROBOTS — WHICH ROBS

WORKERS OF DIGNITY ●

O     5     O

The second illustration on page 100 is a sample of an unfinished cue card for a full-text presentation, unabbreviated. It is incomplete because it has no drawings or underlinings. Notice that the punctuation is exaggerated. Try using long dashes for pauses (and obey them when you come to them!). Your punctuation doesn't have to be grammatically accurate, but it should be speech accurate. If you might pause too long at a grammatically correct comma, leave it out.

Remember, everything must be readable from arm's length. The transition period in middle age during which we begin to need reading glasses can be disconcerting. We need glasses to see our notes, but don't need them (or want them) when looking at the audience. We make the print on our notes bigger and bigger until a short speech uses a hundred cue cards and then give up and wear half glasses in which we feel too professorial. You can buy bifocals with clear glass at the top, but they are hard to get used to. Our advice? Master an outline system using big type. You won't be embarrassed if you forget your reading glasses—which happens at first.

## Should You Use Full-Text or Outline?

There are two ways that you can format your final draft into useful notes. You can present the speech from full-text notes or you may prefer to speak from an outline.

Using full-text means that every word you want to utter appears in your notes and you intend to present these notes without deviation, asides or digressions. This system is best for speakers who are a bit nervous and don't want to leave anything to chance; formal situations in which every word counts (such as testimony that will be a part of a record, or when the speech will be reprinted in the press or in a journal of proceedings); when your topic is controversial and you are in enough hot water already and you can't afford a slip, omission or not-quite-right nuance; when you expect to address this group again and wish to avoid freezing up in mid-sentence (did I tell them this story last time?). And, of course, you'll need full-text notes to present a paper at a conference.

A full-text speaker's energy is freed up for genuine connection with the audience. You are relieved of the burden of figuring out what to say next. The challenge in using full-text notes is to sound fresh and interactive. The audience has come to hear a talk, not a reading.

*Formatting full-text notes.* A full-text speech looks downright weird. It looks unlike any other document you prepare. Use very wide margins (because it is easier to find your place if you are only reading down the page, not also across it). Use a large (18 or 24 point) type size. Start the text at the very top of each page (less than one half inch from the top). This is no time to worry about the lumber shortage; use only the top third of each page. The blank bottom confines the text up high so you don't have to lower your head each time you glance at your notes. It's easier to find your place if you have only a few lines to choose from when you look down. Double-space between lines. Indent each paragraph.

*Using a detailed outline.* For some occasions it will seem both practical and comfortable to use a detailed outline. When a speaker works from an outline, she is prepared yet flexible. When you use an outline you must still write the speech out in full and rehearse it. Then you reduce it to a detailed outline, and rehearse it again from the outline before you deliver it. Detailed means detailed. For example, in this excerpt from Barbara Carson's *All the Livelong Day,* the full-text reads:

> People may hate their work, but even so they try to make something out of it. In factories and offices around this country work is systematically reduced to the most minute and repetitive tasks. Supervision ranges from counting bones, raising hands to use the bathroom, issuing "report

cards'' with number and letter grades for quantity, quality, cooperation, dependability, attendance, etc. Through all this workers make a constant effort, sometimes creative, sometimes pathetic, sometimes violent, to put meaning and dignity back into their daily activity. I realize now, much more deeply than ever, that work is a human need following right after the need for food and the need for love. The crime of modern industry is not forcing us to work, but denying us real work.[8]

Poor outline:

    People hate work, but try
    work reduced to minute
    supervision (examples)
    workers try to put dignity back
    work is human need
    crime being denied real work

The above outline will not serve the speaker well for two reasons: first, she may misunderstand her own shorthand and state that ''people hate to work so they try to reduce it''; secondly, much of the punch of the text may be lost if the speaker can't remember the examples of supervision she had planned to give, or the adjectives (pathetic, violent, creative) that describe the workers' efforts.

Detailed outline:

    People may hate work—but they try make something
    Factories, offices—
    Work systematically reduced, repetitious tasks
    Supervision: counting bones
                 hands bathroom
                 report cards—quantity
                           quality
                           attendance

> Workers' constant effort—creative
> pathetic
> violent
> put meaning, dignity
> Realize work human need—food—love
> Crime not forcing—denying real work

*Formatting an outline.*   The best outlines minimize the number of words running *across* the page (or card) and present instead a vertical list of topics going about halfway *down* the page. This arrangement isolates thoughts visually so that they are easy to pick up in sequence.

## Cue Cards or Paper?

*Using cue cards.*   Humorist Erma Bombeck claims the reason so many speakers prefer cards is that their sharp edges are handy for slitting the wrists if the talk goes poorly. We use eight-by-five-inch white unlined cards, which are larger than standard index cards.

*Carrying cue cards.*   You could use a thick rubber band you can trust not to break to keep your cards in order until you are ready to use them. The technique we prefer, however, will be apparent to the eagle-eyed reader who spotted the holes punched at the *bottom* of the sample cards shown earlier.

The neatest, most convenient, most professional-looking and most foolproof way to use cards is to put them in a binder. When you snap your big index cards into a binder your cards are never out of order, even if you drop them. Don't forget that the holes should be punched at the *bottom* of each card because you turn each card *down* after using it. Best of all, your binder sits on the ledge of the podium, propping your notes up high so that you can see them without lowering your head.

*Using paper.* New speakers prefer heavy stock (instead of ordinary twenty pound paper) for several reasons. If your hands are shaking, the rustling will be less conspicuous if you are holding heavy paper. If you are on a mike, big index cards and heavy paper make less noise. (The wind can still blow unsecured notes away if you are speaking outdoors, or even indoors if a fan is blowing.)

*Carrying paper.* Enclose your presentation in a three-ring binder but remove it from the binder before you begin speaking. If you present your text from the binder, you will distract the audience every time you turn a page. The idea is to brush each

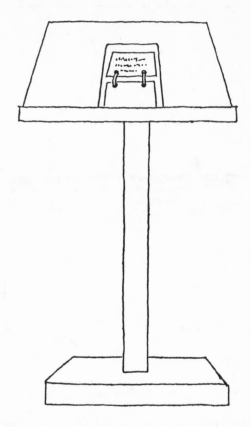

page *aside,* not flip it over. This is particularly important because if you've taken the rest of our advice, you'll have a lot of pages.

## Decorating Your Notes

After you have rehearsed out loud several times from your text or outline, you will get a good idea about where to "decorate" your notes so that your delivery will go smoothly.

*Number every card or page.*

*Go back over the notes with a colored felt-tip pen to enlarge your punctuation marks.*

*Draw body language reminders and other stage directions in the margins.* Don't write words; you might try to read "smile" instead of smiling. Draw a picture in a bright color instead. If your English is accented, be sure to make liberal use of "pause" reminders. New speakers complain that under stress they ignore their drawings. It takes practice to be able to deliver the text and perform the actions your drawings remind you to do.

*Underline words you want to emphasize in color.*

*Draw small down arrows (↓) over your emphasis words.* Adjectives, adverbs and the last word in a sentence should be emphasized down (with a lower pitch) rather than up.

*Mark some of your text for elimination.* If your audience gets antsy or your talk must be shortened due to some emergency you won't have to stop to think about what to cut. Remember that things happen: dogs wander in; the electricity fails; the moderator doesn't have the assertiveness God gave industrial carpet and your turn to talk coincides with the group's loss of patience. Don't take it personally. Be flexible enough to give up some of your beautifully timed, golden words if people aren't able to listen. Some speakers run a highlighter through the "only if I have time" portions of their text; others paperclip pages to signal "this can go."

*Redo any page that is too messy.* If you have to cross something out, cross it out completely in heavy black so there is no chance of accidentally reading what you meant to delete. You want to have clean copy in front of you for delivery.

SMILE

 STOP WAVING HANDS AROUND

 FEET STEADY

 EYE CONTACT

 PITCH DOWN

 LOUDER

 PAUSE

 PAUSE, THEN SPEAK FASTER

 PAUSE, THEN SLOW DOWN

Your final rehearsals should be from the finished version of your notes, with all the drawings, underlings and "ditch this" flags in place.

*Sample final page.* Notice that the double-spaced text starts at the very top of the page. The type is large, the margins are wide and the punctuation is geared toward speaking. Also notice pagination, pictorial cues, underlings, deep indentation of paragraphs and general legibility.

---

It is not for business to mete out what is to be saved and lost on the planet. It is for ecologists to determine what is a sustainable commercial pursuit and what is not.

Adlai E. Stevenson once said a hypocrite is the kind of politician who would cut down a redwood tree, then mount the stump and make a speech for conservation.

Jayne Nelson/Speech to EPA Boston /p. 19

---

By the way, there are psychological advantages to all this mucking about with notes. The more you handle your material the more comfortable you will feel with it. Physically pushing it around seems to help speakers feel in control of their talk.

## Achieving the Appropriate Relationship with Your Visual Aids

The greatest visual aid is a clean speaking environment that is free of distractions. Erase the previous speaker's diagram, clear away the old coffee cups and saccharin wrappers, pull the curtain so there will be a nice backdrop behind you, close the venetian blinds so that the group members who wear contact lenses will be able to see you through the glare.

Most other forms of visual aid are a crutch, a dodge, a distraction. That's why new speakers love them so much. We hope sophisticated audio-visual materials and snazzy technology will get us out of the spotlight, make us appear more legitimate and help us be taken more seriously. Slick packaging and fancy technology won't get us out of our dilemma if the problem is our failure of nerve. We must find the courage to make our words meaningful and thus effective. Use visual aids only if you really need them, if they truly add something beyond stylish veneer.

*Objects.* Keep your "show and tell" items out of sight until you reach the appropriate moment to hold them up. There are shelves built into most podiums—a good place to conceal visual aids. Members of the audience will keep wondering what the object is if they can see it. Better to have them listen to you.

If the object is not large enough for everyone to see, you might as well leave it home. If the group is seated close together, you can pass things around without much disruption, but you also run the risk that each individual will tune you out when it's her turn to examine it.

*Flip charts and blackboards.* To add value, the visuals must be visible, and the speaker must be thoroughly familiar with them. You look like an airhead if you have to stop and study or hunt for the appropriate spot on your chart. Don't write on the blackboard until you have to. Until you're ready to spring it, keep each flip chart page covered up. Write only on every third sheet so that the text from the pages underneath won't bleed through. If you try to write on a flip chart with a marker that is old and faded you will kick yourself for not specifying to the liaison ahead of time that "markers" means new, fresh, wet markers.

*Handouts.* We think handouts make a nice exit gift. If you can't hold off distributing a handout until the very end, at least don't give it out until the second it's time to look at it. Audience members will start reading while you are talking. You may fantasize that people will follow along with you from item to item, but half of those cheaters will probably flip ahead to page seven when they should be on page five.

The other half of the audience will be pointing to items of interest and whispering to each other behind their hands and causing confusion.

*Overheads and slides.* A strong visual device such as slides or film dilutes your personal rapport with the group. It had better be worth it. You must use overhead or slides rather than a flip chart if the group is large—always keep the back row in mind. These examples are typical graphics used at briefings:

An organizational hierarchy
A pie drawing, with percentages represented by slices of the pie
Maps, charts and other graphics
Exact words to be copied down by the group (e.g., titles and authors, names of art works and artists or technical terms)

Overheads or slides are helpful if you have to explain a subtle or complicated process that requires listeners to visualize a long series of actions accurately and/or to remember or even memorize them correctly. Sometimes they are very dramatic, such as the classic 1930 profit chart. If you are giving an art lecture or a scientific paper you probably can't avoid slides.

Are there blinds or curtains? If not, get the room changed or your images will be completely washed out. Does your projector cord's plug have two prongs or three prongs? Do the electrical outlets in the room match? If you discover too late that your liaison was mistaken you will be frantic. *Always bring an adaptor.*

If the information on the screen is more important than your speech, print the visuals in a booklet and mail them. Otherwise, keep yourself center stage; you are the focal point. Don't divide the audience's attention by placing your lectern across the stage from the screen. Situate yourself in the center, and put the screen a few feet to your left. You want to be able to move out from behind the podium, but not wander into the projector light. The projector table goes to your far right. Face the group and *use your left hand for pointing.* Attach the slide clicker to the podium with masking tape, and mark the "forward" button with a marker or a stick-on label. Don't talk to your visuals, face your group.

Structure your presentation so that you aren't constantly having to dim the lights; it takes a while for the eyes to adjust to both dark and light. If an assistant is running the lights and/or the slide projector changer, be sure she has a copy of your text with her cues marked. Practice working with whatever equipment you use so that you are able to find and manipulate all the buttons in a dimmer light, but do not darken the room entirely. If there is no dimmer switch, ask that the two or three ceiling bulbs closest to the screen be removed. (We keep telling you to show up early.)

Shut up every time you do something physical (change a transparency, push the carousel clicker, flip the chart paper, or put up the next chart board). Pause, make the physical movement, reestablish eye contact, then continue talking.

When using overheads, stand at the screen, not at the projector or you will aim your words into the transparencies. To follow your text when you're using overheads (and need to use a pointer on the screen from time to time), position the projector next to your lectern, and move between the screen and the lectern. Avoid pausing at or looking at the projector longer than you need to. Position a transparency, then step away from the projector. Get your eyes back on the group.

Assemble and keep with you a visual aid emergency kit: a clicker cord extension, an extension cord, tweezers to remove jammed slides, masking tape, plug adaptor and an extra projector bulb.

Do not become visibly upset if the technology fails you. By all means ask for help if you need it, but do so in a firm and confident voice. It helps to know the name of the person who can help you. "Kai, the recorder is jammed and we have a frozen image on the monitor." "Maureen, I'm getting a lot of fuzz in this mike." Omit all the "Oh, dears" and hand wringing. Stay in charge.

To sum up, use visual aids effectively by using them only when they are necessary and only let them be visible at the exact moment you need them. Aids must be simple, clear and visible. Keep your eyes on the audience, not on the visual aid. Point to the item on the chart, then keep talking to the group. Hold up your object, but don't look at it; look at them. Before you begin your rehearsals make sure that the equipment arrangements with your liaison person are clear and in writing.

# CHAPTER SEVEN

# Rehearsal and Presentation

You gamble every time you open your mouth. The purpose of rehearsal is to improve the odds that your risk will pay off. The jitters may be unavoidable, but blathering isn't.

Although the speaker/audience, platform/auditorium setting is artificial, we hope you will be the same person behind the rostrum that you are at the breakfast table—except more alarmed and better prepared.

Just as an alcoholic doesn't need to lose her desire to drink in order to stay sober, you don't have to lose your fear before you can do a good job. You can fake it. Our goal should be to perform so well despite fear, that fear gradually dies.

If you rehearse as if you weren't nervous, you will discover that you act pretty much as you practiced when the time comes. Anxiety is always more bearable if you can count on yourself to do an adequate job.

The first time you practice out loud you will either be able to feel the words you have written for yourself or you won't. If you don't feel anything, go back and rewrite.

## Rehearsal

We recommend a minimum of *six timed, stand-up, out-loud* rehearsals. You must rehearse your presentation out loud; a silent rehearsal is no rehearsal at all. If you're giving a twenty-minute speech, this means you will rehearse for at least two hours. A five-minute talk requires a half hour of practice. However, we don't suggest you rehearse all at once. In fact, the further apart you can space your six rehearsals the better.

*Speak loudly and clearly.* Speak loudly and clearly. Speak loudly and clearly.

*Memorize your opening and closing remarks.* You need to be able to say them "eyes up" without using your cue cards as you do for the middle section. You do not memorize a whole speech, nor do you read it. You memorize the opening and the closing remarks and familiarize yourself with the rest so you can use your notes comfortably while making frequent, sustained eye contact with your listeners.

*Rehearse the entire speech each time you rehearse.* New speakers tend to overrehearse the first third of their presentations. In your anxiety, you may only imagine yourself getting up and saying your opening lines. However, you have to say it *all*. Rehearse the *whole* speech until it feels comfortable to you, all the pages look like old friends, and you know your sequence of ideas by heart. If you fluff lines, or leave something out, recover as you would in the "real" speech and keep going. Practice your talk from the beginning to end each time; don't backtrack to repeat something in a better way—you wouldn't backtrack with the group listening. To make each rehearsal count, do everything just the way you plan to with the audience, including recovering from mistakes.

*Rehearse with props.* Use a small table for a lectern. Approximate what your speaking environment will be. Visualize your audience by setting up chairs to talk to. Rehearse your visual aids, too.

*Rehearse in front of a mirror.* Check your body language. If you fidget, or shift your weight from right to left, you will see it and be able to correct it. How much of the time are you looking up from your notes to seek eye contact? If you aren't using a notebook, check to see that you are setting your notes aside when you finish with them, rather than flipping them over.

*Rehearse into a tape recorder.* Ear copy is different from eye copy. You are not interested in how the speech looks on the page. How does it sound? Does it make sense? Does it have life? Do you need to vary your pace, your inflection, your pitch? Do you sound monotonous? Does your voice trail off at the end of sentences?

To practice increasing your volume, put the tape recorder at the other end of the room. This will force you to speak up because the mike won't pick up your voice unless you are projecting it. To speed up familiarization, listen to the cassette while you're commuting or exercising.

A "canned," stilted, "read" sound doesn't come from too much rehearsal. It comes from being afraid. The more you have rehearsed the easier it will be to sustain eye contact with the audience. It is genuine contact with individuals that animates a speaker.

*Time each rehearsal.* If people expect fifteen minutes, they will turn off and tune out after fifteen minutes. It is better to edit a presentation to make it clock out short of the time limit than it is to race through sections of it or to squeeze in too many unexplained ideas. It is better to hear "I could have listened to her all day; her presentation wasn't long enough" than "That thing lasted a year."

*Rehearse in front of live bodies.* You will be less nervous delivering your speech to an audience if you have already delivered it to an audience. You will be more relaxed for the real thing if you set up a mock presentation for your preschooler, your landlady or anyone you can yank off the street to listen. You have to unveil it publicly anyway; lessen your risks by doing it ahead of time.

Ask your guinea pigs for criticism. You may get some good suggestions from objective listeners. If they say there is something they didn't understand, reevaluate.

Since family members and close friends are often the most difficult people to speak in front of, do it! It is a great counterphobic strategy to seek them out. If you can stop feeling self-conscious in front of them you can in front of anyone. Warning: These are the same people who are often the most critical, and you have to *trust your own opinions.* The way you say it isn't exactly the way they would say it. Families are helpful because they know when you're being phony, pompous or stuffy. But beware of family politics, too. Maybe Daddy said it stinks because he's unconsciously threatened by Mommy's growing charisma. Remember, your dog or parakeet is better than no practice audience at all.

If members of your mock audience don't agree with your talk, good! Hear out why. You can then figure out from their objections how to reinforce your argument, and be better rehearsed for the sparks that may fly in the question-and-answer session.

You might ask a friend who can spell and punctuate to correct an article for you. Why not ask someone who speaks well to "audio edit" your speech by listening to you and correcting mispronunciation, malapropisms, clumsy syntax and incorrect grammar?

*Rehearse in your real clothes.* Is the outfit you're planning to wear the day of the presentation comfortable whether you're seated or standing? If the armholes are too tight, you may look rigid and unnatural. Since you *will* smear mayonnaise on your blouse at the luncheon before your talk, you don't also want big, wide sweat stains under your arms, do you? Pin in those dress shields! You may notice in rehearsal (before it's too late) that your jewelry clanks, and your new skirt has a tag hanging from the back you hadn't noticed before. It's ridiculous to worry about your clothes. Spare yourself by rehearsing them, too.

*Rehearse the question-and-answer session.* When you feel adequately prepared for the presentation, begin rehearsing your answers to the questions you hope they don't ask (see Chapter Eight).

*Rehearse success.* No matter how intimidated you may feel, if you force yourself to maintain a positive mental attitude by imagining yourself relaxed, animated and truly engaged with the group you will be taking the wisdom of thousands of athletes, actors and public speakers to heart (see Chapter Three).

## Delivery

Virtually anyone can acquire speaking skills that are adequate and acceptable for most occasions. Many of us can become very good speakers; it is unfortunate that so few of us do. We would like to change that both because we care about the status of women and because we hate to be bored.

Whether you are a first-timer hoping for adequacy, or an experienced speaker striving to lift the audience out of their chairs, you can improve your delivery. Here's how.

*Take your security blanket.* Develop a checklist and consult it before you walk out the door. In your agitation, you may forget to bring a handkerchief, a watch, the names of people who will greet you, directions, your notes, visual aids, a mirror, Tampax, Kaopectate ("Is this what they call 'preparation energy' or am I going to have diarrhea?") sinus spray, aspirin, a paperback book on which to prop your notes, eyedrops, your glasses and business cards. Don't forget extra nylons; the ones you are wearing are going to run. (If your boss is in the audience, both legs will run.) It wouldn't hurt to keep an airline vomit bag in your emergency kit. Women who give a lot of talks not only develop a checklist, they keep a kit permanently packed.

*Establish your territory.* You have arranged to arrive early. All speakers need the bathroom. Your first priority is to discover the fastest route to the "ladies" and determine whether your sadistic host organization compels you to beg a key from the receptionist each time you wish to use the facilities.

Test the microphone by raising and lowering it to the correct height for your mouth (about six to eight inches away). Don't get too close to the mike. You want to stand far enough away from it so that you still have to project. Ask to have the mike turned on so you can figure out how close you want to be. Don't let them adjust the volume so that you will have to speak softly. Remember that when the room is full of bodies the sound will be deadened and you will have to speak up even more.

If you are using a necklace mike, practice looping it around your neck and clasping it so you won't get red in the face and sweaty struggling with the damned thing in front of the group. The same goes for clip-on mikes and body mikes.

*Test the lighting.* Go to the podium, take out a mirror and view yourself facing all directions. If you have light skin and you seem to look sallow, it may be because the lights have an amber gelatin placed over them. Request a pink gelatin instead. Do you want more makeup? Less? Is there enough light to see your notes? Is the little light on the podium too harsh? You can either turn it off, or cover it up with tissue to soften the glare. Does it make you appear cadaverous when you lower your head? Sure it does. Can you see each and every one of your soft, meandering chins when you lower your head? Of course. Now aren't you glad you won't be lowering your head?

*Clip-on mike.*

We've shown you how to prepare and position notes to keep your text—and your chins—up high.

*Try to get accustomed to the setting.* Feel the podium, walk around it. Practice getting to the spot from which you will be sitting or otherwise waiting. Are you going to have to maneuver stairs or cables for mike, lights or video? Practice setting your cards down. Are there any last-minute changes that could be made to the seating arrangement that would help you?

The idea is to feel that you are on home territory, that you "own" the furniture, the stage, the equipment. You know where things are, exactly how they look and feel. Nothing should be strange or unfamiliar—giving the speech is challenge enough.

*Remember that you're "on" before you begin speaking.* The audience will form an impression of you before you even open your mouth, but only partly because of the introducer's words and attitude. The way you act while you are being introduced or *anytime you are visible to the group* influences your reception. Confine your yawning, neck rolls and other loosening exercises to the restroom.

*Display interest in whatever is going on.* If you are nervous, you will be tempted to obsess about yourself. You already know that the trick to a successful presentation is to concentrate on your ideas and your audience. Forget about yourself. Take (or feign) interest in whatever speeches, rituals or announcements precede your talk. A speaker with her nose in her own notes ignoring the group's cherished anthem is a speaker who is asking for trouble.

## Breathe and Affirm

Keep it simple. Your superb preparation means you are now down to only two chores: monitor and control your breathing; and obliterate negative self talk with an affirmation.

*Breathe regularly.* Use rhythmic slow exhalation breathing from your diaphragm. (See the "Modulating Your Voice" section in Chapter Two.) Sit up straight like your mama told you. Take care not to cross your legs (this cuts off your midsection and you need it for breathing). Don't rotate your ankles around in circles. If you make faces to your friends in the audience, don't expect to be taken seriously when you stand up to speak. Move around from time to time, or your assertive yet relaxed image will get blown by muscle cramps.

*Psych yourself.* Choose what goes on in your mind while you wait to be called on. If you fail to take firm charge, the little harpie who lives in the deep recesses of your psyche will start in on you. "Why in hell did I agree to do this? Is it too late to get laryngitis? I look like an idiot in this suit. I should have worn the blue. I probably have a booger." Once started, the harpie can go on forever. Don't let it start. Instead, repeat one or two of the phrases suggested below to mesmerize yourself. Say them like you believe them. Even if you don't believe them (yet), at least keep your desperate mind busy with practical, attitude-adjusting language. Don't allow time or room for thoughts that are scary ("I'll never remember everything") or negative ("I can't go through with this"). Thinking helpful thoughts takes no more energy than thinking hideously self-defeating ones.

Heighten your impulse to communicate by repeating:

"I'm glad I'm here. I'm *glad* to be here."
"I know what I'm talking about, and I am prepared."
"This is fun. I look fine. I'm ready."
"I am calm. I am confident. I am competent."

Remember that you *want* to feel a bit nervous, up, energized; your psych lines are to keep you from letting the good nerves turn to knock-kneed, green-gilled terror.

The stategy for avoiding an out-of-body experience is to sit with members of the audience, talking and laughing until the last possible moment. Shaking hands, rubbing shoulders and having *conversation* makes it easier to stay grounded and real, then transfer (enlarge) the "conversation" to a bigger group. In an auditorium or theater setting, Janet usually arranges with her liaison to have about twenty people from the audience seated in a semicircle of two or three rows up on stage with her, usually to the left of the podium. Sitting amongst and talking with her new best friends on stage before the introduction encourages a continuity of manner (a "speech" is just talking), and makes the transition to talking with a few thousand less artificial.

## A Last-Minute Drill

By now you have stored all your toys (handkerchief, notes, watch, vomit bag and water) in the podium shelves. If you have a pencil in your hand, ditch it. The chances are that if you take it with you to the podium you'll play with it throughout your speech (if not poke yourself in the eye with it).

## You're On!

Your name is called. Your only remaining options are to flee the solar system or give it your best. If you have written a miserable speech, try to pull it out with a good delivery. It is time to *do the best you can with what you've got,* because right now it's all you've got. Go!

Walk briskly to the platform. Do not drag or shuffle your feet; a positive, yet unhurried stride suggests readiness and tells your audience "I'm glad to be here." If you approach the podium as though it were a guillotine (or rush away from it when your talk is over) you communicate distaste for the group and undermine your message.

*Take your time before you begin.* Smile briefly at the group, then settle your notes up high and to the far right or far left. Find a stance that suits you, adjust the mike if you need to, let your arms and hands fall at your sides, or rest lightly at the lectern. Glance at your notes so your opening line will be on the tip of your tongue. Then look up. Face the house for about a count of six (or until they settle down). Radiate warmth and approval as you look them over. Pausing allows you to project a quiet authority and firm confidence. Make sure they're listening before you begin.

*Begin at a low pitch, with adequate volume.* Your first few sentences may be shaky if you are very nervous. Your legs and hands might tremble, and your voice might, too. The beginning is usually the worst time for a speaker's particular symptom (maybe you will experience them all!). Don't worry about this. The last thing you should punish yourself for is nerves. You will probably relax as you go along. Don't be nervous about being nervous. By the time you've reached your conclusion you may feel better.

With practice, you'll learn to accept nervousness as a productive contributor to your presentation. In the meantime, think of your audience as friendly; most people are actually very tolerant of mistakes. Their reaction often takes the form of "I'm glad she's up there, not me." Audiences seldom lie in wait, but are rather sympathetic to the position you're in. Therefore, concentrate on their needs, not on yourself and your anxieties. You are there because you have something to give them.

If this is your first "speech" you may find after it is all over that you went into a trancelike state, and you can hardly remember what happened. The speech goes by like a blur, and it's over before you're fully conscious again. If your talk is tightly organized, lucidly argued and well-rehearsed, you will probably deliver it on "automatic pilot" pretty much as you delivered it during rehearsal. People will listen, and it will be a success. If you have confidence in what you are about to say, your subconscious will feel comfortable with the delivery. We put a great deal of emphasis on preparing well for a presentation because even the worst speaker cannot entirely kill a good, well-rehearsed speech. Of course, an excellent speaker may successfully pull off a virtuoso performance of a shallow speech, too.

If your reaction to the unfamiliarity of giving a report, announcement or briefing is an out-of-body experience, you are likely, once it is over, to be tempted to cut loose and display great signs of relief. Do not throw away your hard work by sighing hugely and rolling your eyes at a friend. Just don't. Save the story about how "it all went by so fast I didn't even know it was happening" for later.

## Volume

Trust the information you get from any member of your audience about your volume. If they say you are not audible, believe them. No doubt, you sound loud enough to yourself. You are standing right next to yourself. Further, you're hearing yourself through your eustachian tubes. Speak loudly and clearly. Speak loudly and clearly. Speak loudly and clearly.

## Posture

The best posture allows for freedom of activity. People sense your confidence, feelings of security, self-assurance, courage and strength from your bodily manner just as they do from your words.

Poise is efficient body movements, gestures that fit the sense of what you're saying. The opposite of poise is random, needless, repetitious or meaningless fidgeting. If you plant your feet firmly, and balance your weight on them evenly, the plaintive cry "But what should I do with my *hands*?" will go away. We are not making this up. Steady your feet and keep them steady. Pepper your notes with foot drawings. Deliberate walking from spot to spot is fine. But shifting your weight from one foot to the other, never mind the array of odd positions which can be assumed by the undisciplined foot, is the source of your arm and hand awkwardness. Trust us. It's true.

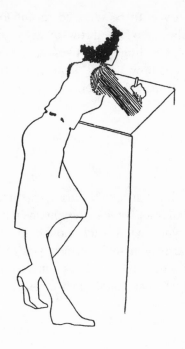

*Stand on both feet.*

## Restrict Movement If You Are Using a Mike

If you have a clip-on, lavaliere or body mike you have lots of freedom of movement. Most mikes, however, are freestanding or attached to a podium. You don't want to move "off mike" so your movements are restricted. You can lean forward on the podium to establish intimacy, or for dramatic effect but do this only once or twice to make a point. Steady leaning makes it look as though you need the rostrum to support a dead body—yours.

Don't keep looking at the mike. It won't move. It won't bite. The ear-splitting electronic whine called feedback, can result from the speaker standing too close to the mike.

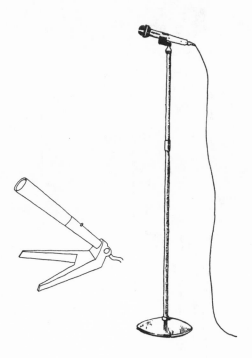

## Restrict Movement If You Are Not Using a Mike

Your goal is purposeful movement, not nervous energy that
results in fidgety, distracting movements. If in everyday life you
have practiced substituting relaxed but controlled movements of
your hands and arms for random, jerky flailings, then you are
bound to appear more poised during your speech. If you don't
have good habits yet, pay attention to the body language drawings on your notes.

Generally, keep your eyes on the audience when you move.
Initiate a movement, such as stepping three paces to the left,
in a lazy fashion and end it lazily. Wait a while before returning
back to the right.

*Meet your audience. You are not tied to the podium.*

Move away from the lectern and toward the audience to emphasize major points. You also can move from one side of the rostrum to the other as you make transitions from one subject to another. Do not pace. The audience will start counting your steps.

## Gestures

Do not invent gestures or plan them. They should be genuine and spontaneous, resulting from normal freedom of action and the absence of nervous movement. Meaningful gestures do not include fluffing your hair, rubbing your knuckles, twisting your ring or smoothing your dress.

## Notes

*Without a podium.*   If you have no podium, hold your notes away from your body and up much higher than your waist. You don't want to obscure your face, but you always want to be able to lower only your eyes to the notes, not your whole head.

Never attempt to conceal your notes. If you are well rehearsed you should have no trouble finding your place unerringly unless you've lowered the notes so far down that you can't see them very well. Without a podium, you'll set each card or page down on a table next to you as you finish with it.

*With a podium.*   Position your notes as high as they will go at the far edge of either the right or the left side of the podium. Set them to the right if your preferred gesturing hand is the right, so it's always free, while the left keeps the pages moving left. If the podium is severely raked, create a false ledge on the real ledge (a paperback book, a box of kitchen matches) so that your notes will remain positioned as far north as possible. The note formatting and note positioning we recommend will enable you to consult your notes by merely flicking your eyes down (rather than dropping your whole head) to find your place. Set each page aside when you are finished with it—most of the space on the podium is liberated for this messy pile since you are only using the far northeast or northwest section of the podium. Do not flip notes over because this is obtrusive and may obscure your face. Do not try to put each card or page behind the stack because you might accidentally slip one back into the middle of the stack and find yourself staring at it again. Brush your notes to the side.

When you have finished speaking, you will need a few extra seconds to stack your papers or cards. Do not briskly gather

*Don't worry if you need a lot of cards or a thick stack of paper.*

your notes together and whack them to bring the edges in line. This is officious. The notes need only to be neat enough to get a firm grip on them so that you don't drop them on the way back to your seat.

*Using a small notebook.* Position the notebook as high as it will go on the podium. You remembered to punch your large index/cue cards at the bottom, so you simply flip each card down when you finish with it.

   In a worst case scenario you will have no lectern or no table. In that case place used cards or pages at the bottom of the stack you are holding.

## Face to Face

For the first few minutes you can limit your eye contact to those faces that seem the most sympathetic and responsive, but after that you have to talk to everyone. People's faces will tell you that they are puzzled, or they can't hear, or that you've gone flat. If you run into a rough patch and get rattled, it's okay to return to the most supportive faces until you've braced yourself.

Your expression should be appropriate to your words. The incongruity of a pleasant smile nullifies the effect of a serious argument. If you are talking about drug addiction or making a serious request don't smile. Also, don't smile if you are so scared the smile looks completely phony. An expression that registers good news and interest is fine too.

Audiences take on the emotions of the speaker. If your face registers joy, they will begin to feel it, too. If you look grim or fearful the audience will absorb it and return it. Why not trigger receptivity by looking at them with enthusiasm and affection.

## Overdo It

Exaggeration in print arouses suspicion. In an oral presentation, it makes a more respectable impression. Speech delivery settings flatten your personality. Use strong emphasis on a stage or in front of a classroom. Your "overstating" and "overemoting" is probably coming across as bland understatement. Your interest in your subject must be avid, and *show*.

## Don't Be Afraid of Silences

"Everything looks like failure in the middle."
—Rosabeth Moss Kantor

If you mess up, shut up until you've recovered. Do not use fillers (ums, deep breaths, waving your hands, muttering, making things up as you go along). It is better to pause and be quiet, to make the audience wait, than to babble. New speakers experience every second of silence as an eternity. Remember that the audience is on real time; speaker time is distorted. Make 'em wait. Unskilled speakers usually read too quickly. Pause for effect whenever your cue cards say to.

## Don't Be Afraid of Noises

People drop things. People cough. People change their seats.

## Pretend to Digress

The group does not want to feel read to; they want "talk." If you are properly rehearsed, you'll come across as though you are departing from your script from time to time (to tell a secret, to say something that just popped into your head), even though you aren't. You will know some sections of the talk well enough by now to do them eyes up and in an "impromptu" manner.

## Handling Questions

You're there to clarify facts that concern you. You need not shrivel up and die when your audience discovers you don't have all the answers. Your concern will provide the emotional energy to make the issue meaningful to your audience (see Chapter Eight).

## Exit Gracefully

Your body language as well as your words will let the audience know you have finished. Don't say "thank you"—just give them a nod of the head then a quick step back from the mike. Gather your notes calmly, looking up to acknowledge the applause, and leave the stage/podium/front of the room the way you arrived—briskly and firmly. You are "on" until you are out of sight completely (meaning back at home, not just back to your chair). If you roll your eyes, shrug your shoulders, sigh, or in any way indicate "God, I'm glad *that's* over" or "Oh, hell, did I ever screw *that* one up," you will wreck the effect of the presentation. You "take back" everything you said by acting relieved or behaving as though you have just play-acted the grown-up giving a talk, and now it's time to resume being a juvenile. You may *feel* that way, but do the audience the courtesy of keeping your misery to yourself. From beginning to end, the *very* end, communicate what you planned, not the feelings you may be trying to overcome.

## What To Do When You Get a Standing Ovation

Act like you deserve it. Without sounding like Pollyanna may we suggest that there is almost always something to be proud of in any speech. After the presentation is over, be good to yourself. Smile if you can manage it and look pleased with yourself. It may not have been the best performance ever but it was the best you could do that day under those circumstances and you are going to get better. Even if you only managed to get out there on your wobbly legs and impersonate an adult, act proud.

## Afterward—Critiquing Your Own Speech

A practical test of how your speech went is to ask whether the audience responded by talking about what you said. Were there questions, objections or arguments in the days and weeks following your talk? Did you stimulate discussion? No matter whether you were dazzling or dull, view your performance objectively. Regret is wasteful. And remember, a next time will come. You have to learn to accept failures in making presentations the same way you accept failures in any other endeavor: recognize your mistakes, learn what you can from them, resolve to do your best not to repeat them, and move on. You usually have just as many witnesses to other failures in life; you are just not as acutely aware of them.

## To Improve

Remember that all speech is public speaking. Speak often. The more you assert yourself in every speaking situation the easier it will become. In fact, you may become addicted to it as we have. The power to communicate, to reach out and share with an audience, to influence other people even briefly is heady stuff. It increases your confidence and that in turn increases your ability—the very antithesis of the exclusion/inexperience/powerlessness cycle that has trapped women for eons. It may not seem revolutionary, when your cooperative nursery school asks you to do an orientation session for new parents, or when your boss asks you to present a report at the next staff meeting, or your church asks you to make an appeal for funds, but it is, it is.

> *"We can do anything we want*
> *if we stick to it long enough."*
> —Helen Keller

# CHAPTER EIGHT

# Questions and Answers

Even if you think your speech went smoothly and you feel proud of your performance, you will probably feel let down if the question-and-answer period is listless. A good speaker wants to parry questions from the audience, the tougher the better.

As we have insisted all along, a good presentation has the air of a dialogue. During the question period the feedback you have been getting throughout your speech from facial expressions, body language and your intuition about the audience becomes concrete verbal response. Ideally, it is time to share the responsibility that has been yours alone up to now.

Questions can be full of peril. This is not the time to lose control or forget what you are there to do—namely, persuade the audience to accept the information you have or the point of view you wish to promote.

Quite often inexperienced speakers visibly relax and become more animated and "real" after the speech itself is over. It is clear they feel relieved. This is more like it, they seem to be thinking, this is the way people really talk to each other. Unfortunately, a radical change in manner undermines what has gone before; it gives the impression that the speaker was putting on an act. If you assume a different personality during the question-and-answer session, either your talk was too stiff or your manner while answering questions is too "I take it all back; I'm just a kid." A marked change may be a danger signal that the speaker doesn't recognize that she is still the speaker, still the focus of attention, still "on." The question-and-answer period *counts*.

And what if there are no questions at all? We assume that when a subject catches a person's interest, she will want to know more. The tradition of question-and-answer periods springs from this assumption. It can be a real blow to discover that we haven't sparked a response from the audience.

To improve the odds against an acute excitement shortage in a question-and-answer period, make sure that there will be questions. You must also understand the dynamics of this speaking situation so that you will parry the questions effectively.

## Making Sure There Are Questions

Pros never go anywhere to speak to anyone without seeding the audience. Talk show hosts on radio and television, politicians and public speakers of all kinds can count on getting good questions because they put them there. They give some friendly person in the audience a question or two to ask if the audience is shy about beginning or whenever things seem to lag. Don't feel hesitant about setting someone up to ask you questions. Anyone will do, a friend or neighbor, or if you are in a completely strange place you can call on your wellworn liaison person. What is the question you would most like to be asked, the question that would really start the ball rolling, the question for which you have a brilliant reply? Plant it.

If there is still a lull after your planted questions, ask yourself questions: "Many of the women I talk to seem especially concerned about combat duty'' or, ''Last week a neighbor said, 'Why do you women have children in the first place if you are just going to dump them into day care?' '' This ploy has to be managed with great confidence and even then is a bit phony. It is a stopgap measure for hard times. Make sure the questions you ask yourself are very hard and nasty ones, otherwise you'll look even phonier. If you find yourself using this technique a lot, go back to the beginning of this book and start over. You are doing something wrong. An audience should have reactions after the ice has been broken. If they don't, either you haven't reached them, or in the case of your own work group, ugly political dynamics are overwhelming curiosity.

Another trick is to laugh and say ''You mean nobody here wants to know about?'' (insert the worst, most antagonistic, embarrassing, hardest question you can think of). In the general laughter and murmuring that follows, one person is bound to call out ''Yeah, I do'' or ''Sure, tell us.'' Pounce on that person and treat your answer as though the question had come from her, from the floor. In timid audiences (high school groups come to mind) nobody wants to go first. If you can make it seem as though somebody already asked a question, others may want to participate.

There are occasionally audiences so inarticulate or frightened that nobody could wrench a response from them. The moment to find out that you have encountered one of these rare audiences is not during the question-and-answer period (see Chapter Four). Prepare for them in advance by asking your liaison, ''Do they usually ask a lot of questions? How have they responded to speakers like me in the past?'' If your liaison suggests that this audience has seldom been coaxed into jumping up and down with eager questions, you can arrange to have written, and therefore anonymous, questions from them turned in to the liaison ahead of time (or, in a longer session, on the break). This is an emergency technique. Use it only when you have strong evidence that nobody is likely to ask the things they really have on their minds for fear of seeming ignorant, for fear of being identified with an unpopular concept or for fear of assuming the role of "speaker" long enough to ask a question in front of the whole group. If the liaison agrees, ask her to pass out index cards to the group as they come in and to collect the questions on them. Go early to choose the ones to which you want to address yourself (if and when the group balks at your other question-eliciting techniques).

You, of course, have done your best to write and deliver a talk that is likely to provoke a response from this particular group, and if you don't stir them you can say, "oh, well" without going home to take it out on the cat.

Difficult audiences, thank goodness, are few and far between. So we will repeat: If you are failing to get questions time after time you may need to rethink your approach. Do not despair. Any audience response is feedback and the purpose of feedback is to help you to make corrections. No response at all is feedback of a particularly dramatic and unpleasant sort; however, be objective: figure out what went wrong and fix it.

## People Will Want to Argue with You

You will never get the following question: "Everything you said was absolutely compelling and my only question is, where do I sign up?" What you will get is a lot of arguments. It is human nature to be skeptical and our natural tendency has been reinforced further through years of schooling. Teacher was always proud when you argued and asked hard, so-called "good" questions because it meant you were paying attention and were interested. It still does. Listen to radio talk shows, or the people at meetings, and especially listen to other speakers' talks. Almost all questions fall into the general category of arguing. There are attempts to show the speaker is wrong by citing new evidence, arguing with the evidence she has used, pointing out inconsistencies, telling long stories about an exception to a generalization she has made and lots of others. This is all benign and never hurt anyone. A smart woman like you with all her facts straight will anticipate other viewpoints and handle these kinds of questions easily. Expect to get an argument; certainly don't be defensive about it.

We would also include under the general heading of "benign questions" such things as simple requests for additional information, fuller explanation of one of your points and documentation of your evidence. The people who make these requests may or may not agree with you, and you may or may not have the answer or wish to answer, but these are all friendly questions. (No matter how upset it makes you to be asked for documentation for a statistic that you just made up in the heat of the moment, the question is absolutely fair; you shouldn't make up statistics . . . now you're stuck.)

## Answering Friendly Questions

Answering a question is a short impromptu speech. The basics are the same whether you are answering questions from behind a podium, during a job interview, at a press conference or while talking about divorce with a five-year-old. As we suggest in Chapter Nine, take your time, maintain your poise and edit to a point. You know more about your subject than your audience does; that is why you are the speaker. Relaxation comes from having considered questions you are most likely to get, writing out answers and rehearsing them. If you have any lingering doubts, get rid of them. You know more and you care about your convictions and you are completely prepared. There may be questions that you can't answer from time to time, but there won't be many.

Maintain eye contact with the whole audience and not just with the person who has asked the question. Unless the question is very simple, paraphrase it before answering so that you are sure you are answering to the point. It is also a good idea to repeat the question because not everyone in the audience may have heard it. For example:

Question: "Are you in favor of prostitution?"

Your paraphrase: "I think you are asking me whether I favor decriminalization of prostitution, that is removing the legal penalties for practicing it. Is that right?"

Question: "Yes."

Answer: "Because blah blah blah, and because blah, yes I do."

Remember to be brief. Think first of your conclusion, support it with one or two reasons, state it and shut up.

Be careful if you are naturally funny; never score off nice people. That means that no matter how witty you are or how moronic the question or how perfect an opening it gives you, you will not say anything that makes your questioner feel stupid or foolish and invites the audience to laugh at her. Remember, you have role authority, you are the expert and you also may be more experienced at talking in public than many in your audience. When you are nervous and unsure of yourself it is easy to dismiss how much power you have standing there behind the podium, but don't forget it and don't misuse it. Never make a person's question the springboard for a joke on that person.

Be succinct. Not everyone in your audience will want to hear the answer to this question and furthermore they have just listened to you talk for twenty minutes and they want a chance to talk, too. Long-winded answers scare the audience into thinking you are about to begin your speech all over again. They may have a plane to catch.

## How to Not Answer a Friendly Question

There may be sincere and well-meant questions that you either cannot or do not wish to answer. If you do not know an answer, don't guess. If you are well prepared you can usually steer the questioner toward an appropriate resource even if you don't know all the facts by heart. For example:

> "I don't have the statistics on Chicana heads of their households but you can find them in the Women's Bureau of the Department of Labor Handbook on Women Workers."

Here's another example:

> "I don't know the percentage of abortions obtained by women whose unintended pregancies occured while using birth control. The last study I saw said 43 percent but if you want exact, up-to-the-minute data, try the Alan Guttmacher Institute or the NOW Task Force on Reproductive Freedom. They'll know."

It is a good idea to announce the limits of your area of competence before and during a question-and-answer period. If you have come to talk about safer sex, you do not want to answer questions concerning career opportunities for the mature woman, and you don't have to no matter how relevant the question may appear to your questioner. If it is possible to pave the way for an answer that you do want to give, then do so. The beauty of vague or open-ended questions is that you can answer as you wish, make your own point. Otherwise, just say, "That's an interesting question and one I'd love to discuss, but I'm not qualified to give you solid information on it." Or, "That's a good question, but it isn't what we are talking about right now; I'd prefer to reserve this time for questions about _____ ."

There are also irrelevant questions that you do know the answer to but don't want to waste your time with. This happens frequently with reporters and talk show hosts who don't know what to ask because they haven't done their homework (see Chapter Twelve). Ilka Chase once said "If once in a lifetime you find yourself up against a stupid group, don't let them know that you think so. That stupid they are not." This is excellent advice.

There are also questions that are not even questions but just somebody in the audience making his or her own speech. The trick to dealing with these is to steer the asker toward a question you do want to answer. For example:

> Question: "I have this elderly woman friend who gardens a lot. She was out in her garden the other day and got so sunburned that we're really concerned about her. Don't you think that older people should wear hats?"

> Answer: "Probably. I think that gardening is a good example of the kind of work women who have been in the home for many years ignore when they start the career counseling process. When asked what we like to do, many of us fail to include gardening, sports or civic activities that may tell a great deal about what we like and what we're good at."

If the questioner in this case has tried to go on and on about taking her friend to the hospital and about the callous doctor and how hard it was to find a parking place and so forth, you must interrupt. "Will you state your question, please?" Do not allow members of the audience to make speeches. It is bad enough when they are boring and irrelevant or inaudible, but it becomes downright dangerous when such speeches are unfriendly.

Never be fooled into thinking that because it is such a small, warm group you can answer indiscreetly. Treat every question as though your answer will appear on the front page of tomorrow's paper. It just might.

Finally, there are friendly questions that you don't want to answer because it would take too long. Just say so. Indicate briefly the direction your answer would take and invite the person to stay after the presentation to discuss the matter with you, and then move on. Be brief. Let your people go.


## Hostile Questions, Hostile Audiences

A casual opponent is a person who has heard more arguments against your opinion than for it, and asks for information in a challenging, though not closed-minded way. These questions, however chilly, still fall within the limits of rational and "friendly." ("I believe you mean what you say, but I'm not convinced. Who else says so? Give me some more examples.") Audience members who strongly disagree with you may still be civil as well as curious.

Then there are hostile audiences and hostile questions. It's important to draw this distinction because if you are so nervous and defensive (many of us are) that any reaction short of total affection makes you furious and tearful then your first encounter with a *really* hostile audience will probably kill you and we wouldn't want to be liable for failure to warn. Try to head into the question-and-answer with a few reminders to yourself that although you may be hungry for approval and love, you will survive if you don't get it here.

It is important to make sure you do not mistake reasonable disagreement for malignant attack. The distinction is not always immediately clear because people are not usually completely open about hating you. We think it is safe to say that certain kinds of questions are inherently hostile. Any question based on a stereotype about your size, sex, race, religion, sexual orientation or age is probably not going to lead to fruitful dialogue. (For example, alcoholic Indian questions, money-grubbing Jew questions, dumb broad questions, impotent old man questions and a zillion others will tip you off that the asker is hostile.) You will notice that there are a great many stereotypes about a great many kinds of people; women aren't the only ones who suffer. You should notice this so you won't become bitter and twisted before you have given your third speech.

Questions about your personal life are almost always undermining unless your personal life has been your topic or the audience is very young. Young people have a great curiosity about how grown-ups live, eat, sleep (and with whom), got their jobs and so forth. Young people try to find role models and it's probably all right for them to ask, but it's not anyone else's business.

You can say "I would prefer not to answer that question," and go on to the next one. You do not have to defend your preference or explain it. Our era of sleaze journalism and "tell all" approaches to public discourse has normalized even the most rapaciously intrusive inquiry. We say personal questions are improper. Your public does not own you. Besides, your answers to invasive inquires can always be used against you ("What does she know, she's so young, so old, divorced, not divorced, rich, not rich," and so on).

Trick questions show you to be a dangerous fool or an evil corrupt influence no matter how you answer them. The discrediting point of the question is buried in such a way that you may not catch it at first. For example:

> Question: "A woman like you probably hasn't had any trouble, but don't you find that many customer service reps *sympathize* with the customer's situation?"

Unless you confront the buried attack you have been had. The questioner has planted in the mind of the rest of the group the notion that you are such a cold bitch you couldn't possibly grasp the emotional pressures and conflicts experienced by others.

Another example of a trick question is one with a false assumption or two hidden in it. Look at these two examples:

> Question: "There is no homosexuality in the animal kingdom but you seem to think that humans, who are, after all, animals, can go against nature without harm."

> Question: "Since women are now on a level playing field with men at work, isn't their lack of advancement into top jobs simply a reflection of their weaker career commitment?"

The hardest part of formulating a response is trying to decide whether the buried false assumption is a trick in itself. Is it an attempt to obscure your message by sidetracking you into an argument that is silly and irrelevant? We have had animal kingdom discussions up to here and don't really want to do it again, but on the other hand if others in the audience really believe that animal behavior is exclusively heterosexual, then maybe . . . and so on. You have to steer a fine course among tiresome red herring discussions without allowing too many false premises and misconceptions to go by.

Last but not least are insults so sugarcoated that they are hard to locate at all. The Smile and Screw school of question-posing includes all the friendly condescending help you get from people whose compliments make the point that you couldn't possibly know what you are talking about.

> "If all you lovely young lawyers would take into account the statistics on. . . ."
> "I think you did a terrific job with your little chat just now and I. . . ."
> "You couldn't be expected to know this, but. . . ."

Any implication that what you think and say is uninformed or trivial should be confronted directly. Since each woman has a different style, the "right" comeback for one woman won't work for another. For example, the speaker could interrupt: "What do you mean, 'little chat'? I'll have you know that was a jumbo speech. Now what is your little question?" in a humorous fashion that would make her point without making an enemy. The same approach will fall flat—or insult—if it is not consistent with the speaker's personality.

## Answering a Hostile Question

The first step in dealing with a hostile group is one you should take before even leaving the house. As we pointed out in Chapter Four, it is critical that you have background information on your audience before you go to speak. If you are sure that your topic always stirs up bile and decibels and that the group is going to disagree with you, then you can prepare yourself psychologically. The object is not to work yourself up into a defensive rage; in fact, it is just the reverse. Before you begin, try to care about the feelings of the people who are going to disagree. It is your responsibility to set the tone of this "meeting of the minds" so you must be objective, friendly and reasonable yourself or all is lost. That is very hard especially in the heat of discussion after people have been attacking you. It helps to psych yourself ahead of time. Repeat one hundred times, "They are uninformed and don't understand; they're frightened; they hate what I stand for, not me," and so forth.

Most of us think of ourselves as nice people, very ordinary conventional folks who just happen to think executive compensation is excessive and are going to talk about it to some nice people from the American Management Association. We have a tendency to be surprised and injured when we are attacked as dangerous radical crazies because, to us, our position seems eminently reasonable. If it didn't we wouldn't hold it.

The point is, don't be surprised when people go after your credibility and ego. You may think you are psychologically prepared, but unless you have encountered a hostile audience before you probably aren't. Don't worry if you aren't sharp and witty and brilliant in your first encounter. Nobody is. Most of us are cowed, upset and hurt. You get used to it, and before you know it you are handling it like a pro. You are not likely to convert a prejudiced audience so sometimes the best you can hope for in writing and delivering your presentation is to keep things on a rational friendly level and take care not to offend with a careless remark.

It is easy for us, of course, seasoned by controversy, to blithely tell you to get a rabies shot and not worry. The truth is that only experience makes it easier to stay in charge of yourself and of the situation. Experience thickens the hide and builds your confidence and also helps you to realize that the worst that can happen isn't much. So go out and get experience. Start with small, friendly groups if you can and work your way up to your company's leadership team, which is still wary about whether your job in the Human Resources Department should even exist. Get yourself to Toastmasters. Trim your speaking engagements to how strong you think you have become. If you have never given a talk before and cry easily, don't start by delivering a presentation advocating twenty-four-hour-a-day child care on demand (to be paid for with the money we save cutting the defense budget in half) to the American Legion Post 876 of Smalltown, Indiana.

Now for the specifics of handling hostile questions.

*Ask for clarification.* When the audience is angry it becomes even more important to understand exactly what they are asking you. While it is fine to ask "What do you mean?", don't do it when you know perfectly well what awful things the questioner is asking/saying. Then your "What do you mean?" becomes transparent avoidance (based on the shaky hope that the questioner will hang himself by elaborating). It works better to confront the situation and say what you think.

*Paraphrase.* "If by 'x' you mean 'y,' then my answer is "_____ ." "Let me repeat the question back to you in my own words to see if I understand it."

*Slice the question down to size.* Divide up questions, especially those based on several misconceptions. Try saying "I can't answer your whole question, but if part of what you would like to know is _____ my answer is _____ ."

*Change the subject.*

> "That is an important issue, but in my judgment it is not the critical issue. I think the critical issue is _____ ."
>
> "That's certainly one area of concern. Another is _____ ."

"That's a good point, and I think another important consideration might be _____ ."

"I don't believe we have enough time for me to comment on x, but I would like to say something about y, which is related."

*Disagree.* Feel free to say "Let me think a moment," before you plunge into dangerous territory. Express understanding of the remark and then give your opinion: "I can certainly see how you might come to that conclusion. Many people have. But here's what has persuaded me otherwise: _____ ."

Partially agree with the response if you honestly can: "I agree with what you said about _____ ; but I don't think I can agree with your observation on _____ ."

> Buncombe, n. 1. Insincere speechmaking intended merely to please political constitutents. 2. Insincere talk; claptrap, humbug. Also, bunkum.
> —*The American College Dictionary*

*Be honest.* This cannot be stressed too strongly. We have had it up to here with voodoo statistics, B.S., material omissions and flat untruths. An audience senses when you are fudging an answer and they will not like you any better for doing it. Aim for respect. If someone asks you why you solicited campaign contributions from the folks who illegally dump radioactive waste in our waterways, don't claim you didn't know that the company wasn't "green" and expect to be believed. We both know that's horse patoole and so does the audience.

If someone in the group points out that you have made an error of fact, stand tall and say, "You are correct, and I was incorrect."

*Do not cave in to confrontational demands for a "yes" or "no" response if a one-word answer is untruthful.* The questioner does not want to leave room for reasoning, but if your real answer is "it depends," then don't accommodate him.

*Do not theorize, speculate or talk abstractly.* Stick as closely as you can to your own experience or well-documented evidence. Offer as little room for argument as possible. Unless you want to have a shouting, shoving brouhaha, don't bring up speculative abstract issues. There may be a few who will argue with you if you say "I am deeply religious." There are many who will argue if you say "Deep religious feelings are all that distinguish human beings from other animals." Similarly, it is hard to argue with the fact that the Department of Labor says that 45.5 percent of the work force is female and this figure is up from 29 percent in 1950. It is easy to argue violently with statements like, "It won't be long before all women work their whole lives just like men."

*Avoid falling into an exclusive dialogue with one nasty person.* Listen attentively to the question, but while you are answering it, shift your eye contact to the audience as a whole. Don't answer more than one question from a person who doesn't like you or your answers. The best strategy is to invite other questioners: "I'd like to hear from some of the rest of you."

*Pleasantly short-circuit ill-timed questions that interrupt the flow of your argument.* Try "I've left time at the end for dialogue. Please hold your comments until I'm through, then I'll call on you first." "I'd like to finish answering questions about salary-leveling before we move on to questions regarding employee ownership of the company."

*Prevent speeches from the audience.* A questioner should be allowed thirty seconds or so to fully develop a question if it is complicated, but should not be allowed to make a speech. Interrupt the usurper by holding up your hand in a "stop" or "time out" gesture, then say, "So that we'll have time to hear questions from a number of people, would you please state your question."

*Don't score off questioners.*   Most of the time an agitated hostile question comes from someone who represents the fears and concerns of others in the group. You will not win friends by using your superior wit to destroy this person. Even the most dismal boor deserves your courtesy because you have the advantage. You are the speaker, you are the powerful authority. He or she is speaking from the floor, without introduction or formal legitimation. If you use a putdown, the audience will feel sympathy for your victim and not for you. The only time this isn't true is when one individual monopolizes the question-and-answer period and makes everyone mad. When you manage to shut the speaker up, the audience will be grateful.

*Do not try to shout down hecklers.*   If the heckling is just getting started and is sporadic you can say that you plan to stop speaking unless the heckling stops, but it might not work. The liaison person, organization chairperson, program director or whoever can appeal to the crowd to behave themselves; that is not your job. Hecklers who refuse to allow a crowd to hear a speaker because they disagree with her position are sometimes brought to heel by the crowd, but don't count on it.

There is no clever trick to dealing with serious heckling. Don't even try to deal with it. You are obligated because you have taken the platform to put up with an audience's ignorance and their fear, which they may express in the form of honest anger, but you owe no one an apology for refusing to accept abuse. Shouting back won't help, witty remarks won't be heard and people who might be reasoned with about the injustice of heckling won't be the ones who are doing it. Make a calm announcement to the effect that you cannot and will not speak under the circumstances and leave. Period.

Do not be concerned if you were prevented from speaking; the hecklers' behavior is their responsibility. Yours was to arrive prepared. You met your responsibility.

## Wrapping Up a Question-and-Answer Period

As we pointed out in Chapter Five, a weak conclusion can ruin a perfectly good talk. Remember that the question-and-answer period is part of your speech and bring it to a strong conclusion. Women who have been brought up to be responsive and accommodating will often go on bravely answering questions far beyond a reasonable time to stop simply because people are still asking them. It isn't rude to cut questions off. You must stop when the end has come and stop decisively. How do you know when?

A typical speaking engagement runs about forty minutes, with twenty minutes or so for the speech and twenty minutes for questions. Unless you are in a workshop or very informal fireside chat where lengthy discussion is appropriate, twenty minutes is plenty of time to field questions, so after twenty minutes, *stop*.

At the risk of belaboring the obvious, the best time to stop is before the audience runs out of questions. It makes you look bad to say, after waiting hopefully, "Well, if there aren't any more questions, I guess I'll step down." Wistfulness is not the effect we are striving for. As soon as the questions stop coming thick and fast (three or four people with their hands up at once) it's time to quit. Don't beg or look disappointed. Always leave while people still want a little more.

Alert the group that you have only a brief time left but don't say, "I can take one more question." What if the next question is terrible? If possible, call the halt just after you have answered brilliantly and not after you've been forced to hedge or say you don't know. Remember, this is the conclusion of your speech. Make it count.

Speakers say things like "I'm afraid we're going to have to stop. It was a pleasure talking with you," because they didn't prepare a *better* one- or two-sentence closing for the question-and-answer period. Smile, acknowledge the applause, put your notes together and step away.

Leave time for private questions. There will be members of every audience who prefer to ask their questions in private after the speech. While you pause to be thanked by the liaison person, let your motions be slow and relaxed so those who wish to approach you will feel that you are accessible. Warning: sometimes a person who comes up afterward will want to monopolize you for another hour or two recounting their life's story. Don't feel obliged to listen beyond a brief question or two. Heart-to-heart talks are appropriate only if you feel like having one, which you probably won't, having just spent an intense hour on stage. Turn to someone else. If there isn't anyone else just say that you must go, and go.

# CHAPTER NINE

# An Introduction Is A Speech

*"Mommy, this is Jamey.*
*He eats frogs."*

## Social Introductions

The purpose of a social introduction is to tell people enough about each other so they can begin a conversation. Etiquette manuals advise us to say the name of the ''senior'' person first. (''Madame President, this is Jane Elioseff.) The ''senior'' person is defined as the one who is older, of higher rank. When women and men are being introduced, the woman is to be named first.

We think these conventions are ageist, sexist and snobbish. We feel uncomfortable with introductions that dwell on the individual's rank, status or ''importance.'' Try to describe others in ways that don't promote categories of ''who matters and who doesn't'' or ''the somebodies and the nobodies.'' An egalitarian introduction focuses on information two unique individuals might like to share with each other, without emphasizing a hierarchy of authority or power between them. Most of us feel more at ease when we hear what we have in common with someone we are meeting for the first time.

Never say, ''I'm Mrs. Lewis'' or ''Ms. Lewis'' or ''Miss

Lewis." Always say "I'm Louise Lewis." It is rude to call yourself by your title. If people need to know that you are a doctor or that you prefer to keep the relationship on a courtesy title basis, then signal this in other ways. On the telephone, for instance, you can say, "I'm Louise Lewis. Please call me Lou. What do you like to be called?" In the unlikely event that the answer is "Mr. Swine," it is wise quickly to add, "Ah, then please call me Ms. (Mrs., Miss, Dr.) Lewis."

If you know the other person's name, the introduction can go like this: "Hi, this is Louise Lewis, Mr. Allen." If Mr. Allen calls you Louise after you addressed him by his surname, you have two choices. If you don't mind making the relationship informal, as he has indicated he wants to do, then begin at once to use his first name, too. If you don't know it, ask. If you prefer to keep the relationship formal and that is what you meant to indicate when you called him by his last name, make your intention even clearer by saying at once, "Perhaps you didn't hear my surname. I'm Ms. Lewis, Mr. Allen."

Titles among adults should be reciprocal. Do not allow *anyone* to first-name you unless you are first-naming back. Similarly, invite people to first-name you—or use your surname—whenever the initial signals are unclear. Eventually we feel comfortable saying things like, "Couldn't we keep this informal? I'd like you to call me Madeline," or, "In business situations I prefer to be addressed as Ms. Barker, Mr. Perot."

If you don't know how to introduce someone, ask, "What shall I say about you?" and then give her plenty of time to think of her answer.

## Shaking Hands

Extend your hand automatically to *anyone* to whom you are being introduced or to anyone to whom you introduce yourself, regardless of age, sex or circumstances. (Shake hands with children, with people on the street, at casual gatherings and, of course, in business situations.) You go first; if you take the initiative the other person won't have to do an agitated two-step wondering whether a handshake is appropriate. A firm, brief handclasp while looking into the eyes (not down at the hands) of the other person establishes you as someone who wishes to be friendly *and* to be taken seriously.

## Introducing Yourself—Your Oral Resume

Most of us would rather not talk at all than have to introduce ourselves to strangers, especially to an audience of them. Furthermore, it's difficult to sum ourselves up in a thumbnail sketch.

An effective sound bite about who you are is tough to invent on the spot, so figure out a simple, brief oral resume in advance. What do you want them to know—and remember—about you?

You will be glad you strained your brain to come up with a "handle" every time you walk up to a new face at a party, go unintroduced before an audience or don't know your tablemates at a training session. If you're afraid you might not care for the way your host may introduce you, it is your responsibility to suggest a two-sentence description she or he can use.

Your social self-descriptions have probably consisted of your name and your reason for introducing yourself into the situation. For example:

> "Hi, I'm Barbara Haber. I live in the white house on the corner and I just stopped by to say hello and welcome. I've lived around here for years, so I can probably answer questions you might have about the neighborhood."

Rethink both your business and social self-introduction habits. Whether you're at a ball game, the supermarket, at a trade show or on an airplane, it does not hurt to tell strangers your key skills and/or your goals.

When a job interviewer says "Tell me a little something

about yourself,'' you get about two minutes to answer before she starts firing questions. This is a speech. Focus on a couple of key skills. Be prepared to support each of the principle strengths you claim. Use anecdotal evidence of your achievements using those strengths. Focus on knowledge you've acquired in the last five years. Touch on your immediate objectives as well as long-range goals in your career development. Explain what motivates you and what you want to be able to say you have contributed when you retire.

## When You Are Introduced as a Speaker

When you introduce a speaker you do your best to make her sparkle. Why let yourself down when you are the speaker? How you are introduced creates an impression that may last throughout your talk; do justice to yourself by making sure the impression is one that will help, not one you have to overcome—or correct—before you can launch into your talk. There isn't a speaker alive who doesn't know from bitter experience how difficult it is to rescue credibility from a miserable introduction.

*Take charge.* Don't just find out what your introducer plans to say about you ahead of time; help her! If you don't, and she's lazy, she'll read your bio (or heaven forefend, your resume or *curriculum vitae*) to the audience. Offer her a written introduction, tailored for the talk, as a draft or a sample of what you think would work. With luck, she'll use it verbatim. At the very least, offer suggestions (a quote or a story) to give her a ''handle'' on the talent, knowledge or experience that qualifies you to make *this* speech.

Look alive during everything being said from the podium; you appear unattractively self-centered if the first time you glance up is when you hear your name mentioned. Keep your ears—and your expression—perked up for all the group's announcements and the previous speakers.

## Introducing a Speaker

If you are obligated to show up for the conference/retirement party/sales meeting anyway, you might as well take advantage of the opportunity for visibility and get yourself a speaking role. Introducing speakers will begin improving your name recognition outside your own group, as well as give you access to decision makers. Like volunteering to make announcements, introducing speakers gives you a relatively low-risk way to build skill and confidence as a presenter and, in the process, makes it easier to get to know a wider array of people informally.

As you read through this chapter you will notice that you prepare an introduction as you would prepare any other talk. Find out about the audience, make arrangements with the liaison person (although often the introducer is the liaison), edit the introduction (preferably with the assistance of the speaker herself), time your out-loud rehearsals, and memorize your opening and closing lines.


## Interviewing the Speaker

As a courtesy to the speaker and as a safeguard for you, contact the speaker well before the day of her presentation. A pro will offer you not only publicity material and a bio, she'll probably be positively relieved to send a sample/draft introduction tailored to the talk your group has asked her to give. An experienced speaker will often suggest excellent quotes, colorful facts or descriptive language you can use in her introduction (that is, she may have a good oral resume). Do *not* trust anything you read about your speaker in the newspapers. Check out all information coming from *any* source other than the speaker herself.

Run through the entire introduction you are planning with the speaker to double-check for accuracy or duplication. If you don't, you may ruin your speaker's opening. For instance, if you choose to explain in your introduction that Sarah Hendrickson, a well-known doctor, is a bicycle expert you might say, "You may be surprised that she will be speaking today on bike repair, not on why bike riding is healthful!" What if Sarah's opening line is something like, "You may be surprised that I am going to talk about bike repair rather than the reasons bike riding is good for our health." Ouch.

## What Do You Say?

Always give your name, her name, the occasion and her topic (even if this information is printed on the program for the audience to read). You will usually say how long she will talk and whether she will answer questions when she has finished speaking. If you are lucky you can include a funny quote or startling fact. Ask the speaker if there is something gripping you could use in your introduction that time constraints required she cut from her speech.

## Be Brief

Whenever we hear someone announce, "Tonight's speaker really needs no introduction," we want to say "Good! Sit down!" If you must precede your introduction with "housekeeping" announcements, make it snappy. The audience came to hear the speaker, not the introducer, so don't remain on stage for a disproportionate length of time. On the other hand, don't repeat the old saw "Well, you came to hear her, not me, so I'm going to sit down now." Avoid self-deprecation in any circumstance.

The introduction to a five- to fifteen-minute speech should take from thirty seconds to one minute. For a main speaker, or someone who will be speaking for twenty minutes or longer, one and a half to two minutes should be ample to arouse audience attention and curiosity without stealing the speaker's thunder. Other than the Nobel Prize ceremonies or political conventions, we cannot think of any circumstance that would justify an introducer hogging the limelight for longer than two and a half minutes.

## Must Do's:

Follow these rules whenever you introduce a speaker.

*Repeat the speaker's name several times.* Be sure to say her full name at the beginning of your introduction, then repeat her name at intervals. Repeat her full name at the end as a cue to speaker and audience alike that your introduction is over.

*Get the name right.* Ask the speaker what name she prefers to be called. Do not assume that Dr. Joanna Rankin wants you to use her title. Perhaps she prefers to be known to *this* group as "Joanna." Practice pronouncing a difficult name with the speaker until you can say it correctly. It is not funny to mispronounce a person's name, and less amusing still to tease or joke about it.

Be especially careful about using first names. Robin Lakoff says,

> I feel that, other things being equal, there is greater likelihood of hearing Gloria Steinem called "Gloria" by someone who does not know her very well than of hearing Norman Mailer called "Norman" under the same conditions. . . . This usage is perhaps to be compared with the tradition of calling children freely by their first names. . . .[9]

*Include anecdotes and quotations.* A chronological recitation of accomplishments and credentials is boring and flavorless. Give the speaker a personality. With her collaboration, delete a few degrees, jobs and honors. Tell a story to illustrate what kind of person she is, what she actually does all day, or what impresses you most about her. Quote her, if possible, or quote someone else's remarks about her.

## What Not to Say

Sometimes the speaker's personal relationships or physical appearance can be relevant information for an introduction. If you are introducing a speaker at a Weight Watchers meeting, her dress size may constitute a "bona fide occupational qualification" for this particular speech. If you are introducing the woman whose daughter is the first girl to play Little League in your town, and your audience is the Women's Athletic Association, then perhaps your speaker's status as "mother of" may be appropriate information.

But, in general, do not describe a woman in terms of her relationships (wife of, secretary to). Tell about what *she* does, not what her husband does or what her supervisor does. Women often resent having their credibility undercut by being defined derivitively, in relation to others.

## Don't Praise the Speaker's Speaking Ability

Wouldn't it make you nervous to hear about what a terrific job you are going to do? How inspiring and hilarious you're about to be? Fame is not a characteristic of the speaker; fame reflects the mood or taste of the press more than it reflects the speaker's good traits or hard work.

## Don't Overpraise

An introduction that states "I'm glad you are with us" is fine. A gushing introduction embarrasses everyone. Maybe you do feel "honored and privileged to be on the same platform with Arlie Scott," but if you carry on about it, your case of the "humbles" may cause the audience to squirm, or perhaps even resent the speaker enough to resist her ideas. ("If she's so much better than we are, so bloody superior in every way, then what's she doing in the company of such simple peasants in the first place? Is this a charity call?") This is an example of how *not* to introduce a speaker:

> "We're so *lucky* to have Steve Manymachos with us today (fawn). He is unbelievably kind to take time out of his busy schedule of important meetings to come and talk to us (simper)."

Glowing words delivered in a matter-of-fact tone are not so effective as a few simple words spoken sincerely. The spirit of good feeling counts the most.

## Keep Yourself Out of It

The audience doesn't need to know your pet opinions on the speaker's topic. Your relationship to the speaker is probably not relevant, either. Who cares if you've known her for twenty years—are you bringing it up to bask in her reflected glory? The exception to your low profile as introducer might be when the group knows and trusts you, but is suspicious of the speaker or her topic. In these circumstances it is nice to say "I'd like to introduce my friend . . . ."

## Rehearse Your Rituals

Whether the speaker is new and nervous, or an old hand at public appearances, tell her in advance exactly what is going to happen and what the sequence of events will be. Tell her what the last line of your introduction is so she will be ready to come forward. If you are planning to shake hands, say so. *She* may be planning to have both hands full of notes and visual aids. Besides, if she isn't expecting a handshake, she may not see your extended arm and both of you will look awkward.

## Don't Stare at the Speaker

Turn only once or twice toward the person you are welcoming. Remember that you are addressing the audience, not the speaker. Just as new speakers sometimes stare at their visual aids and forget the audience, new introducers sometimes gaze at the speaker while addressing remarks to the group.

## Cue the Audience

Let the audience know when it's time to clap. Do this by selecting words that are final-sounding, inflecting your voice in the wrap-up, delivering your final line "eyes up," from memory and using body language that signifies a change. You also cue the audience by repeating the speaker's name at the end, and initiating the applause for her.

In casual settings, take a step back from the lectern or the head of the table when you've completed your remarks, and clap for a second while you watch the speaker approach you. Leave to take your seat after this pause.

In formal situations (a banquet, a large audience, a stage setting), applaud until the speaker reaches your side, shake her hand in welcome and quickly return to your place. Although it may seem strange to shake hands with a speaker you've spent the last two hours with over dinner, and who is also your best friend, do so if the occasion is formal.

## Sample Introductions

Sometimes an introducer is asked to perform miracles. What if your inexperienced speaker tells you only that his name is Justin Jacobson and that he is a student at the University of Oregon. What can you do if you have no resume, no bio, no publicity materials and no oral resume? Try open-ended questions to uncover key phrases:

> "How would someone else describe you in one or two sentences?"
> "Is there something about you hardly anyone knows that you would like more people to know about?"
> "How do you see your role as a _____ ?"
> "Ideally, what do you want to happen/come out of this speaking engagement?"
> "What are you talking about? How did you get interested in it?"
> "What's the best/worst/strangest experience you've had with it?"

Eventually he or she will come up with something funny or unusual that you can use to add color to your introduction.

Now let's compare two introductions of the same woman to the same audience to see how the introducer's motives alter the wording. The group is gathered for a regular monthly meeting of federal employees. About thirty people assemble with their lunches in brown bags to hear speakers talk about issues of interest to government workers. There is ample advertising in advance. A well-worn format dictates how long speakers will talk and how long they will take questions from the audience.

The speaker has told you her name and her topic, "The Upward Mobility Program and How It Works."

| *Full name* | "Barbara Harris eventually sees herself as a community worker in Roxbury, dealing | *Her credentials to this group. In this homogeneous gathering, every-* |

|  | particularly with teen-age children. Her current job as an F.D.A. file clerk won't get her there, but her studies in sociology and psychology under the Upward Mobility Program will. | *one will know that F.D.A. stands for Food and Drug Administration)* |
| *Cue to clap* | Let's greet an ambitious and far sighted colleague. Barbara?'' | *Name repeated. Informal gathering, first-name basis* |

The purpose of the preceding introduction is to qualify the speaker in a way that will encourage the audience to identify with her. She is established not as upper management coming down from on high to pontificate about what the program is supposed to do, but as a worker who knows the reality behind the rhetoric because she is *in* the program. Our excitement about hearing her stems from the enthusiasm we all feel for a success story, one that could be our own someday.

The following introduction is more formal. The introducer appeals to our consumer instincts: is the program a gyp or does it work?

|  | "This afternoon we are going to hear the truth about the Upward Mobility Program. | *Startling, loaded words for a* |
| *Why we should listen* | We have all read the directives regarding what the program is supposed to do, but today for the first time we have a speaker who is qualified to tell | *tame, stuffy group.* |
|  |  | *Special occasion; attention-getting* |

Credential — us what Upward Mobility is actually achieving. Barbara Harris is with the Food and Drug Administration. *Her full name*

What to expect — Her ambition is to become a community worker dealing with teenagers in Roxbury. Before the question-and-answer session, she will talk to us for about fifteen minutes about how Upward Mobility may—or may not— help an employee change career ladders. *Name repeated. Note full name and courtesy title; authority desired. This cues audience to address her formally when asking questions.*

Cue to clap — Everyone join me, please, in welcoming Ms. Barbara Harris.

Here the introducer establishes the ground rules for this group in terms of time and format. Otherwise, the information in this introduction is the same. It is the mood that has changed. This second introduction acknowledges the audience's informed skepticism surrounding Barbara Harris' topic while establishing the image of Ms. Harris herself as a somewhat tough-minded insider who is to be taken seriously. The language is more formal, and the introducer has taken pains to create a sense of occasion for the audience and to make the experience of listening to Ms. Harris seem special. The mood is less warm than in the first example, and while Ms. Harris could praise or blame the Upward Mobility Program, some curiosity may be aroused about which she will do.

## Introducing Panel Members

Moderating a panel can be a real challenge to your ingenuity. Your goal is to dream up four or five introductions that have life, provide meaningful information, treat each panelist equally while accommodating their different personalities, and resolve the problems in establishing several speaker/audience relationships (see Chapter Eleven).

## Why So Much Fuss Over Introductions?

The spotlight may be on you only for a moment, but introductions are excellent practice for larger speaking parts. A series of ninety-second introductions will teach you a great deal about writing to be heard, rehearsing so it counts, improving your delivery skills and managing your nerves.

Introductions also are a prime vehicle for visibility. As the introducer, you have an opportunity to establish rapport with groups with whom you want name recognition. And you also have an opportunity to build rapport with the speaker! Regardless of whether the speaker works for your organization, rubbing shoulders with her may work to your advantage.

# CHAPTER TEN

# Speaking Impromptu

Any time you talk "off the top of your head" you are making an impromptu speech. An impromptu speech is any utterance, no matter how short, which is totally unprepared and spoken without notes. The definition probably shouldn't include what you say in a job interview (bone up!). The definition does include what you say when someone springs criticism on you, what you say to the pharmacist, what you say when you find out your lover has been cheating, what you say when your horse wins the race, what you say when your roommate tries to beg off her turn at the weekend cleaning, and what you say when a coworker unexpectedly asks you for a date.

But, you say, that means I'm making impromptu speeches all the time, every day of my life. That is exactly right. Of course it matters more in some circumstances than in others that you sound intelligent and stay poised; an unscheduled meeting with your thesis advisor is quite different from a schmooze with a casual acquaintance. Nevertheless, those who care about how they talk all the time do better when it really counts.

The ability to speak clearly and effectively without preparation is probably admired more than any other speaking skill. In our classes, it is always this skill students refer to when they say, "She is so articulate." We all fear that in important circumstances we won't be articulate, but will blank out or stumble around. Actually, once you begin to use a "conclusion-organization" technique, "winging it" becomes easier.

The trick of impromptu speaking is not being able to think fast, it's being able to decide, to commit yourself fast. You must decide which of the many things that pop into your mind you actually want to say and the best way to say it. Whatever you decide, commit yourself firmly and irrevocably. This isn't easy to do. Unfortunately, some of us have been so squelched, disparaged and teased that we actually believe we can't think of a thing to say. For example, if the speech you would like to make in response to an interviewer's question about your child-care arrangements is "What's it to you, you stupid jerk?" then it isn't surprising that you think you don't have anything to say. In fact, a different version of that response is a perfect answer, but if you block the original thought you'll never work up an appropriate way to express it. Whether it is because we're afraid of sounding foolish, or because we know for sure our listeners aren't going to like what we have to say, doubt and worry ties our tongue. Often we end up trying not to say what we want to say and our sidetracking, backtracking and "tact" make us sound very confused. Commit yourself to saying what you think. Impromptu speaking isn't difficult because you are dim, it's difficult because you don't have enough confidence in your opinions.

And while we are attacking common misconceptions about being "articulate," let us also say that impromptu speaking isn't difficult because you are under- or mis-educated. All too often in our classes women report that their fear of impromptu speaking (and therefore of networking situations) is based on an underlying uneasiness about their education. Many of us have an exaggerated respect for education and what it can do, perhaps because until recently women were denied access to it. In any case, there is no direct connection between years of education and eloquence. While we would be the last to deny that the best way to become glib is to receive an Ivy League education, ease and confidence come from the experience of feeling entitled and respected (the experience of being treated as one of the elite, a future leader of the world) and not from the books. You can be eloquent with simple everyday words. It is feeling and conviction that make a speech moving. For example:

"No, I won't do it. I don't want to."
"I won't listen to what you say about her, she is my friend."
"Please, help me, I'm afraid."
"I am very angry."

If you want to improve your vocabulary the place to begin is among your friends. Most of us abuse our relationships by talking "lazy" when we feel comfortable. "Wow, I really had a nice day. I had the nicest lunch with Mack Moore, you know, at that nice place on Elm Street. It's just so nice there, really fabulous." It doesn't take an expensive education to treat your friends better. While big occasions often call for the simplest language, everyday life could be greatly enlivened by an animated vocabulary.

When you are unprepared, it is absolutely vital that you maintain poise, which means relaxed posture, audible voice, good pitch, direct eye contact and *no apologies*. Don't say that what you have to offer might not be to the point or won't make sense. Any audience will forgive more if the speaker maintains her poise. If your poise and self-control are superb you can stand still and say "I don't know," and give people the impression you're brilliant, and furthermore, what you don't know isn't worth knowing.

However, appearing confident can take you only so far if you want to *say* something. It is important to have an organized mind. Organization depends on proper structure. Just as you need specific equipment to organize an office (file cabinets, Rolodexes, shelves), you need a framework on which to hang your random darting thoughts. We suggest the following.

Think first of your conclusion. Knowing how the speech is going to end is a comfort to those of us who are scared and good discipline for those of us who would love to go on talking forever. In addition, if everything you say leads toward a conclusion, that alone is organization. A conclusion, a point, a focus, a punch line, is vital.

This approach is not "natural." Most of us try to organize our talk through a chronological order or, worse, simply pile on evidence as it occurs to us. The order in which things happened in time provides simple organization for certain kinds of stories, folk songs and jokes. It is boring, though, and lacks focus. The order in which events occurred may not be the most interesting aspect of the events. "And then I . . . and then I . . . and then I . . ." describes what you did but not who you are, what you want or what you mean. People arrested at the chronological level respond with the "then, then, then" approach to any topic, no matter how little it lends itself to this treatment. For example:

> Question: "Tell us a little about yourself."

> Answer: "Well, I was born in Arkansas, but then I went to New York. I got a job as a file clerk for Time, Inc., and then I was promoted to secretary with some research, and then to researcher and then. . . ."

> Question: "Do you like carrots?"

> Answer: "Well, I used to like carrots but then I had too many at once and now I don't like them much."

> Question: "Would you introduce the speaker?"

> Answer: "Eleanor Bowen is the speaker tonight. She used to be on the PTA, then she got elected to the School Committee and she is going to tell us about closing the schools."

> Answer: "Mary Fillmore is the speaker tonight. She used to edit scientific publications, then she ran the national Federal Women's Program at E.P.A., and now she is going to tell us about how to train mentors."

Your listeners shouldn't have to struggle to understand why

you are saying what you are saying. If people often say, "What's the point?" or "Get to the point," you probably need to practice focusing. *Hit your central point first and hit it hard.* Get to the lead quickly. (Saying, "Get to the point!" is also a put-down. If you know you *are* getting to the point and this person interrupts you often, it is time to have a private word together.)

How can the examples just given be focused more effectively? Begin by asking yourself, "What is the most important thing about what I am going to say?" In the first example, the point is whatever it is about you that you would most like the questioner to know. Let's say this is a job interview with a publishing house. You want them to know about your interest in and experience with books. You might focus in this way:

> "All my life I have loved books as a reader. Now, after five years' experience in publishing, I am highly skilled at the process of putting books and magazines together. I think of myself as a book mechanic."

Many questions call for a "yes" or "no" answer, or an "I'm for it" or "I'm against it" response. First, support your conclusion with your reasons:

> "I overdosed on carrots once *(reason)*. Besides, they are sweet *(reason)* and thick *(reason)*. I hate them *(conclusion)*."

In the case of an introduction, it is important for the audience to know why the speaker has come:

> "Many of us have been troubled by the city's decision to close several elementary schools because of declining enrollment. We are pleased, therefore, to have Eleanor Bowen from the School Committee as our speaker tonight. She will be able to answer many of our questions."

> "Many of us have been troubled by the "catch as catch can" way we nurture the talents of our junior scientists. Mary Fill-

more, of Changing Work, has installed successful formal men-
toring programs at an array of scientifically oriented
organizations like ours. We are pleased, therefore, to have Ms.
Fillmore as our speaker this morning.''

An alert reader will have noticed that the conclusion, while
thought of first, is spoken last. This order makes excellent sense
but is almost never followed. Most of us eagerly announce our
conclusion first and then go on to try to support it. Unfortunately, those who disagree with the conclusion don't stop to
listen to our evidence but interrupt or just tune out. If you put
your reasons for thinking what you think first, you have a better
chance of getting a real hearing and persuading people.

A "conclusion organization" means that you state one or two
quick pieces of supporting evidence and then the conclusion. A
conclusion organization helps us avoid talking ourselves into a
corner. We have all been in circumstances or moods when we
felt so inadequate and humble that we go on and on apologizing
and explaining until we are exhausted.

"Gee, I never really thought about it. I don't uh, well, I guess
I believe that, uh, suicide, I mean, this is sort of simpleminded
but I guess I really think it's wrong, you know? Well, maybe
not wrong, exactly, but not fair. You see, I. . . .''

That speech, accompanied by a lot of shrugging, grimacing
and a little laugh at the end doesn't convey strength and conviction. Don't be afraid to stop, even if what you've already said
is awful. You probably can't redeem it by going on and on. It
doesn't matter who is making you feel inadequate or how or
why; if you are in the habit of making your point and shutting
up, your lack of confidence won't show as much. Clarity and
brevity are easier when you have your conclusion firmly in
mind.

In impromptu situations you can begin with a dull remark,
or a generalization that allows you to stall for time. Your priorities are to think of a conclusion and some supporting evidence.

Before you open your mouth, think about your conclusion. Let's say you quickly decide that your conclusion is "I think suicide is wrong." Begin with a generalization while you compose your reasons.

> "There are so many young people taking their own lives *(generalization)*. But suicide extinguishes hope *(reason)* often in cases where time and maturity would have changed everything *(reason)*. I believe it is wrong."

People will jump in with all kinds of arguments about who should be able to commit suicide and special circumstances and what do you mean by "wrong" and so forth, but you *have* gotten them to listen to your reasons. If you simply say "I think it's wrong for kids to kill themselves," someone will surely shout "Which kids? How can you say that?" and you will end up on the defensive. Save the conclusion for last so you can build your case on your own terms.

Although it may feel artificial and stilted, it is helpful to begin your impromptu speeches with "Because . . ." until you have retrained yourself. For example:

> Question: "Do you favor the Supreme Court decision on abortion?"
>
> Answer: "Because birth control is still unreliable and difficult to use, and because unwanted children are a personal tragedy and often a financial burden on the taxpayer, I certainly do favor the Court's decision."

With practice, "Because . . . because . . . therefore . . ." will become silent. Soon you will routinely arrange your ideas in a well-organized, persuasive fashion. First, use a general remark to buy time. Then, follow the "because, because" format. Finally, give your conclusion.

A longer, prepared speech can work on the same "evidence before verdict" principle as a short impromptu speech. You have a major point to make. Each supporting point can have

supporting points of its own. You may add three or four subtop-
ics and stay fairly well organized. It is impossible, however,
for most people to speak effectively for more than five minutes
or so without some kind of notes. In situations like meetings,
long telephone calls, or interviews where you may wish or be
asked to speak at length, have a notebook with you so you can
make quick notes.

Better yet, make your speeches as un-impromptu as possible.
Think through ahead of time what is likely to happen and make
notes. For example, if you plan to attend a meeting to discuss
the preservation of a local historical building, ask yourself: Who
is going to be there? What will their positions be? What are
the arguments pro and con likely to sound like? Then prepare
yourself by writing down the points you think are important
and practice saying a few words about each. If you get into the
habit of preparing yourself, you can virtually eliminate the
whole idea of impromptu speaking. (The term for speaking with
few or unmemorized notes but with plenty of preparation is
"extemporaneous.")

To get started learning the conclusion-organization technique,
try our list of topics and practice short impromptus until you
are good at it. Do it out loud. It is too easy to sound terrific in
your own head. (When something brilliant that you should have
said comes to you *after* it is too late to say it, make another
impromptu statement out loud.) Topics that come up in conversation all the time include:

> money
> crime
> motherhood
> sickness and death
> the defense budget
> the energy crisis
> the job market
> prices of goods
> transportation

When you practice, concentrate on topics that always give you trouble:

> What to say to the man who is putting his swinish hands on you
> What to say to a friend who hates and attacks another friend
> How to say a few words about yourself (see Chapter Nine)
> How to get the landlord, who never fixes anything, to fix a broken heater
> What to say to the arresting officer
> Or to the thirteen-year-old babysitter who always wants to let you know later whether she will sit on Saturday night
> Or when your lover's mother calls
> Or when your husband has started to call you "Oh, Harriet, for crissake . . ."
> Or when your five-year-old asks, "Mommy, will I ever die?"

Let's take the landlord example. Start with your conclusion. Probably in these circumstances your point is some sort of mild threat, perhaps that you are going to talk to a lawyer. Give one or two reasons and your conclusion.

> "Mr. Smith, when I got up this morning there was ice in the toilet. My daughter has had a cold all winter. It is against the law not to provide heat, and if I am not warm in one hour I am going to call my lawyer."

(You don't have to have a lawyer to say this; you can always get one if the landlord refuses to turn up the heat.)

An enormous vocabulary isn't necessary. You don't have to be original and clever. If your message is short, to the point and spoken without apology, stumbling or embarrassment, you'll be persuasive.

Your first reaction to a topic with which you are utterly unfamiliar is probably to keep quiet. That's a good idea sometimes, but at other times you are forced to speak. For those special occasions you must learn the fine art of subtly changing the subject. Try some "gliding over" phrases like:

"That's a good point and we could also think about. . . ."

"I'm glad you asked because it gives me a chance to talk about. . . ."

"That reminds me. . . ."

Simply launch into your own topic and ignore the subject offered you. Many politicians abuse this technique and dodge more questions than they answer. We do not suggest that you bullshit people. There are circumstances, however, when it is better not to be obedient to a demand for information (see Chapter Twelve).

The wonderful thing about impromptu speaking, as opposed to formal speaking, is that we have lots of chances to practice and can become expert quickly. You don't have to go looking for opportunities to improve; they will come looking for you. For the perfect opportunity, see Chapter Eleven.

# CHAPTER ELEVEN

# Talking in Groups

*"We are perfectly capable of resolving conflicts in other ways than killing each other. The only weapon we can use today is this—the larynx!"*
—Dr. Helen Caldicott

"Is this meeting necessary, or would a party do just as well?" is the first question to ask yourself if you are in charge of a group. Meetings are called ostensibly to inform people or to decide something. Actually, these purposes are often only the pretext for getting together. The real reason may be to rub shoulders, to give the appearance of action or to give the boss a chance to lord it over everyone.

The woman who ignores the human needs of the participants when she arranges and chairs a meeting does so at her peril. You must allow some room for stroking and fun. If you don't, the proceedings will be disrupted by whispering, joking, socializing, arguing, people bringing up the same point over and over, interrupting or asking for unnecessary discussion when the time comes to decide.

Your objective is to be effective on two fronts: to get tasks accomplished and to satisfy the affiliation needs of the participants.

## How to Run a Meeting

When decision-making is not spelled out according to rules that all can see, it may be based on some very strange dynamics. For example, who is the loudest. Or who never says anything but is sleeping with the loudest.

Since most formal gatherings (such as the House of Representatives, school boards, plenary sessions at large conferences) use *Robert's Rules of Order,* we suggest that you familiarize yourself with them. (Professional parliamentarians sometimes conduct classes in the procedure.) Parliamentary procedure can be manipulated to block the wishes of the great majority, to embarrass someone who makes a technical error or to prevent someone from getting a hearing. The purposes of parliamentary procedure (to protect the right of the minority to voice opinions and to prevent hasty action) are sometimes distorted. Those who don't understand the rules seldom get their motions voted on and passed.

Many meetings are boring, inefficient and last longer than they need to. Almost any system of preparation and order is better than none. We recommend the techniques in *Making Meetings Work* by Strauss and Doyle. At the very least, establish rules for introducing topics and for taking turns in speaking.

At many meetings the majority of the attendees don't even know what the meeting is supposed to be about. This is inexcusable. Half-informed members can only reach half-baked decisions. A group needs to know ahead of time which matters will be under discussion or up for a vote. Agendas should be distributed in advance so that everyone will have a fair chance to mull it over and to add ideas. Once a group votes to approve the agenda, the chair is justified in saying, "That will have to wait until another time." "That" is anything not on the agenda. Whoever has appointed herself efficiency expert of the day can also ask from time to time, "Could we try to stick to the agenda?" If there is no agenda, this person, as well as many other quieter people, will be angry and frustrated.

The emotional tone of the get-together may be determined at the moment you decide whether to scatter people in a huge hall or pack them into a conference room. People, like molecules, heat up when compressed. If you want the issue to be cooled down, spread out. If you think there is apathy and you want to generate excitement, crowd. If you notice chattering or a tendency to shift from topic to topic, ask yourself if the setting is too informal. If you want to make sure people in a large group in an auditorium can hear one another, you will need a microphone handy in each aisle.

Training sessions, quarterly meetings and so forth should be held far enough away from your ordinary place of business so that those who fancy themselves vital to some other proceedings can't run in and out to check with the office or make calls. Distance from the job site is particularly crucial when those attending the meeting are not very powerful and are likely to be called away at their boss's whim.

Unless record keeping is highly inappropriate—in revolutionary cells, groups of bank robbers, secret deals, international spy rings—insist on a public record. (In formal groups the recording secretary also takes official minutes of all formal motions, resolutions or decisions.) It helps people to think more clearly if the agenda, meeting progress, main ideas, and pros and cons of the discussion are visible. Flipchart paper tacked up around the walls, or even a good blackboard everyone can see is an improvement over somebody's private steno pad. Visible record keeping discourages rambling, repetitiveness and quarrels by making group activity clear.

## Opening the Proceedings

When you are in charge of a meeting it is up to you to set the stage for fruitful discussion. That means you must take charge forcefully. It will not do for the chair to shilly-shally about. Practice your opening remarks. This is a speech. Introduce yourself, make a few orienting remarks to start the group thinking about the problems at hand, and open the floor. Probably the least welcome words in English are "Well, why don't we all introduce ourselves." The inarticulate hemming and hawing of twenty or more self-introducers will contrast sharply with your superb oral resume. You have read this excellent book and practiced.

Name tags and table tents are splendid, especially if the names on them are in large black letters and are legible from across the room. However, when members of the group are still new to one another, ask each person to announce who she is each time she speaks.

## Running the Show

A well-defined question often answers itself. Before the group charges into solutions, be sure everyone understands why there is a problem. In many meetings everyone votes and goes home mad before the question or the issue is ever properly defined. It is your job (as chair, team leader, meeting facilitator or whatever) to get the issues defined. "Do we agree the problem can be defined as . . . ?" A meeting called to grapple with an issue that is eventually defined as a nonissue is still a fruitful meeting.

> "Josephine has stated that the condition of the front lawn bores her and is not a proper matter of discussion for this group. Do any of you care to take a different stand?"

Ask questions, summarize often and keep the ball rolling. You maintain efficient deliberations by crystallizing contributions, agreements and points of conflict.

> "So far, I have heard suggestions that we cover the lawn with horse manure, that we reseed it and that we pave it over. Does one method seem more practical?"

> "We've heard permanence, parking space and swift results in

support of the proposal to pave over the front lawn. Is there further comment?''

(The recorder, meanwhile is summarizing the discussion for the group.)

A good chair is impartial and encourages participation by remaining neutral at the helm. If you cannot stick to the role of unbiased facilitator, let someone else take over the chair while you enter the debate. Your job is to facilitate a convivial interchange of ideas and differences, not to be a central speaker yourself. Piloting a meeting means motivating others to contribute, and it sometimes takes plenty of self-control to play the waiting game. Try, ''Do any of you care to elaborate on the view that horse manure is expensive?'' to get the group talking. If you wait long enough someone will speak up.

If a participant offers an unsupported opinion, you can ask, ''Can you give us your reasons for that statement?'' Or you can cue the others that an argument bears evaluation by saying, ''Phoebe has offered a broad generalization. Is there any discussion?'' This may prompt someone to request Phoebe's evidence or reasoning.

Remember a rushed conclusion only forces you to rethink the issue. ''Apparently we approve of the suggestion to cover the lawn with horse manure. Before we bring the matter to closure, I believe we should test the decision by discussing the consequences or weaknesses of the idea. Are there any negatives or downsides we haven't thought of?''

People like to go away with a formal ''finished'' feeling. Even if the conclusion of the meeting is obvious, it is still the chair's job to state the exact results anyway: the areas of agreement, the areas left unsettled and the plans for action.

Make a clear, specific statement of all promises by all parties. (''We've reviewed all the options, and agree on Operation Manure. We can start in two weeks. Is that agreeable?'' ''Fine, we've agreed that on Tuesday the 14th, Maury will . . . , and by the 19th Katie will . . .'')

# Troublemakers

People go to meetings for a variety of reasons, not all of them helpful to the task at hand. Meetings are attended by professional negatives who are anti-everything and by grandstanders who want to provide a running commentary on each point. Neglected, confused, sullen or withdrawn members may become disruptive. Look around, watch people's faces and see if you can head off trouble before it starts. If someone is shaking his head violently, say, "You don't seem to agree, Douglass. What do you think?" Draw out those who are reluctant to speak up unless invited. They often have something valuable to contribute.

You also must quiet a domineering pushy member of the group who talks all of the time especially if he or she isn't listening to what anyone else is saying.

> "James, I'm going to acknowledge the other raised hands before you or other previous speakers talk for a second time."

> "Alexi, will you explain how your remark relates to the agenda item? We are considering item four. Are you addressing that point?"

There are also people in every group who will enthusiastically and pleasantly address every single question *at length* unless curbed. It is sometimes easier to summon the nerve to silence a participant who is clearly overbearing than to silence a nice person who is simply overeager.

It may help to have a private word with the person who takes up too much floor time: "I hope you will understand my dilemma. If I am not successful in eliciting the participation of everyone, I will not have done my job. Please hold off on your contributions for the rest of the day, and let me see if I can't get the others to speak up. I appreciate your enthusiasm but I don't want to get a reputation as unfair." Here is another approach: "If I am not successful in eliciting the participation of everyone, I am afraid you will wind up doing all the talking and thinking and possibly all the work as well. Please hold off on your contributions for the rest of the day. I want to see if I can get the others to speak up. I appreciate your ideas, and I don't want the group to become too dependent on you."

Then there are the Smilers. It doesn't take much experience to learn that the woman who listens with a tight little smile on her face and who never objects to what is being said may be the woman who will try to undermine a decision or backstab a presenter indirectly, manipulatively—and definitely after the moderator or speaker is out of sight. A Smiler in a one-shot audience is best ignored. But if you meet the Smiler again and again (as in a class you teach or a group you chair), then it is necessary to encourage her to state her objections openly. You can then negotiate, or persuade, or perhaps be convinced that she is in the right. If you discover that she will not embolden herself sufficiently to speak up, even with encouragement, you must neutralize her negativity in another way. Get her to state publicly, "No, I have no objections" or "Yes, I agree" or "No, I have nothing to say." A person who confines her disagreements to after-the-meeting criticism discredits herself. It becomes obvious to the group that she is two-faced or does not have the courage of her convictions. Her peers will eventually react to her private displeasure with, "Well, why didn't you speak up?" or "But you were asked what you thought."

## Creative Listening

Clearly, nothing of value is going to be accomplished unless people listen to one another. Terrible disruptive quarrels break out because the combatants didn't hear or misheard one another. When we hear the entire implications of someone's idea, we don't scream "You're crazy!" because we usually find *parts* of the idea valuable—or at least concur with some of the values and reasons behind the idea.

Acid exchanges result from permissive procedures. When the chair refuses to allow participants to speak out of turn or at cross-purposes, there will still be disagreements but there won't be war. In extreme cases it is necessary for the chair to remind everyone that it is acceptable to attack issues but not people. State that you will not tolerate coworkers (group members, the sisters, whomever) getting personal, interrupting, calling names or using a disrespectful tone of voice.

When you moderate a volatile group or when the issues have aroused strong feelings, insist that nobody quarrel with another person's opinion until the objector has paraphrased that opinion to the satisfaction of the speaker. As a participant, do not answer an objection yourself until you are sure that you are speaking to the real concern that is being raised. For example:

> "I think if we allow that sort of thinking to influence our decision then we have taken a serious step."

> "Franklin, I think you are objecting to a certain point of view but I'm not sure what sort of thinking you mean."

> "I mean the so-called liberal point of view, which tries to solve problems by throwing money at them."

> "You mean we may be planning to spend more money than we have?"

> "Yes."

> "Well, I believe Judith is prepared to show all of you some of the budget figures for 1996–98 that have been projected. . . ."

Most of us go haywire when we hear insults, tags, labels and other nasty ways people have of objecting to what we have to say instead of listening to and answering the objection itself. It doesn't really injure your position after all to have your opponent call it "fascism" unless you then enter in with "knee-jerk liberal," "bleeding heart" and so forth.

## Making Your Presence Felt When You Are Not in Charge

Women—because we are newcomers to power—feel the pressure to be correct, while men feel much freer. Notice how men tolerate each other's unfocused statements of hasty judgments while a woman sits silently, caring that what she says be "right."

Speak up early in every meeting. In fact, abide by the rule of three: speak first, second or third, but don't hesitate any longer. The longer you wait to talk the more you may feel that what you say has to be brilliant or profound or perfectly timed. You can't concentrate on what the others are saying while you sit there trying to get up the nerve to speak. Once you have spoken it is easier to speak again. Say something neutral, early in every meeting until speaking begins to get easier for you. For example, ask to have the blinds closed, or for an extra copy of the agenda, anything to start speaking. If there are five people in your group, try to do one-fifth of the talking.

A good part of being effective is achieved by becoming visible. Are you trying to take up as little space as possible? Spread out, relax your posture and make sure you aren't allowing others to encroach on your table space in meetings: spread your papers and other items out, too.

You may feel safest schlumping down beside your oldest and dearest friend, but the action may be elsewhere. Make yourself uncomfortable and sit down next to the influential instead. Notice where the power sits. Integrate the space; don't let all the "decision makers" clump together. Plunk yourself down where you'll be hard to ignore—probably the middle of the conference table. The action is in the direct line of vision of the person

*This poor woman's body is so wrapped up, she* can't *speak.*

whom you most wish to impress, persuade or influence. At briefings, speeches or large meetings when top management is in the front of the room, sit close to the front yourself. Force yourself to overcome the old school habit of lurking in the back.

Bosses love to hide behind large pieces of furniture. Nothing can make you feel like an accused murderer pleading with a judge faster than trying to talk across a wide expanse of mahogany. Move your chair right up next to theirs.

Is the room too cold? Are the dynamics impaired because people can't hear, or are seated too far from one another? Say, "Is anyone else cold? I'm going to turn up the heat. I see empty seats up front. Why don't we all move closer so we can hear better?" If you get the creepy feeling that *nobody is* in charge, assert yourself. Do not sit politely by while the chair allows people to go off on tangents. Share leadership responsibility; offer process suggestions if the topic is jumping around, if the moderator fails to insist that speakers take turns, or if the proceedings are being stifled by mindless bombast and prattle. Do you notice that members of the group are consistently missing excellent points because they don't like the person who is making them (because her style is abrasive or she expresses herself shyly or she offends the group's dress norms or because she has been stereotyped by reputation)? Speak up!

Is there more action at the door than at the podium? Say, "I see latecomers bottled up at the door. I think it will be less disturbing if we stop for a minute to welcome them and wait for them to get settled." Others will be pleased if you speak up about a situation that is bothering everyone. And, finally, resist the pressure to conform. You don't want to leave a meeting thinking, "Why didn't I push for it—it was the right idea."

## The Sexual Politics of Floor Time

We know that boys are called on more often in school and talk more in their average responses, yet when teachers are shown films of classroom discussions in which boys outtalked girls by a ratio of three to one, the teachers still perceive the girls as talking more.[10] We are so culturally trained to think that women should be good listeners that we are perceived to be talking more if we talk equally.[11]

> *"Many women do want to listen, but they expect it to be reciprocal. I listen to you now, you listen to me later. They become frustrated when they do the listening now and now and now, and later never comes."*
> —Deborah Tannen, author of *You Just Don't Understand*

You are probably sick of struggling for attention at the conference table you fought so hard to reach. The failure to elaborate, to question, to discuss a woman's idea—to simply ignore it—is commonplace. Topics or suggestions we initiate are dropped with a grunt; our points are ignored. It is hard to keep throwing out ideas that are not volleyed, contributions that are not acknowledged.

Men seldom simply respond. They often either wait until a woman finishes talking then say what they had planned to say all along without reference to what she has just offered, or put her through an ordeal of over-scrutiny—picking, picking, picking at her idea. (Similarly, a man attempting to achieve dominance will exercise stare privilege; if he is already content with the degree of power he has over her he'll look away when she talks).

In *You just Don't Understand,* Deborah Tannen says that men simply aren't interested in the concept of taking turns. It is harder to concentrate on the interconnectedness of problems or the value of ideas when your priority is achieving a competitive edge in the group, or more control. Intimidating, directing and protecting a superior position causes lots of noise but little real connecting.

There are two tasks before us. First, to support each other's efforts to make ourselves heard without copying styles we don't admire (such as issuing fiats, aggressive joking, interrupting, status mongering).

Second, we must remind ourselves and each other that the way we are treated probably isn't personal. Nearly twenty years of studies in sociolinguistics and psycholinguistics show that men are intensely focused on establishing themselves and improving their position within their pecking order. Their jousting matches, their proving of points and scoring off each other—and you—probably has nothing to do with the quality of your contribution. But if much of what you say is ignored, trivialized or argued to death, the temptation is to become a bully . . . or silent.

Instead, calmly protest when anyone interrupts you. Interrupt interrupters. "Senator, I don't believe Ms. Thill has quite finished." "Larry, Marcia is talking; we want to hear what she is saying." Keep your eyes fastened on the woman who was talking—if you turn to look at the interrupter, you acknowledge that he has the floor, and you give your consent to his interruption. Reserve your attention for her until her turn is over. If you don't catch on to the fact that someone has usurped the floor until after the fact, you can still say, "I didn't get all of what Amy said because Bill interrupted her. Amy, will you repeat what you were saying a while ago about the Literature Department?"

Sometimes we try to protect ourselves against interruption by filling our speech with pads. "Mmmmmmmm, hm, let me see, aaaaaaah" is one way to signal that you haven't finished your thoughts. There are more effective ways, however, to hang on to your speaking turn. When you allow your eyes to drop to your lap someone will inevitably try to interrupt even if you make "stalling" sounds. If someone tries to interrupt while you collect your thoughts, look at him squarely and lift one hand in a gentle gesture to indicate that you do not wish to relinquish the floor. Or say, "I am not through. I want a second to think."

We may either disagree or build on what a woman says, but if we don't respond to each other much of what we say will fall into the abyss. Don't let a woman feel she's put her point into outer space. Pick up on it, acknowledge it, recognize that she has spoken. Encourage women to talk. "Hold it a sec, Bill, I believe I saw Amy shake her head. Amy, did you have a comment?"

The chair can say, "I want to get full participation from everyone. Please hold on until others have had a chance to comment." If a woman offers a point and the next speaker takes off in a different direction say, "Is this where we want to be going? We seem to have digressed from Amy's point." Or, "Ralph, I suggest we take that up as soon as we finish the subject at hand, which is Amy's suggestion that. . . ."

Provide one another with opportunities to speak. "Carol Dine has had more experience with this than most of us. Carol, do you have any suggestions?"

Men's less constructive behavior is usually rooted in their sense of entitlement and motivated by conscious and unconscious concerns about hierarchy—am I one-up or one-down?—and control. But motive (benign or malignant) is entirely beside the point when the value of talking together as a group is undercut by repeated interruption, asymmetrical length or number of talking turns, the appropriation of others' ideas as one's own, habitually taking oppositional stances, non-listening and fake listening.

An excellent step toward improving the present state of sexual politics is to initiate and sustain a dialogue about ways to achieve healthier group dynamics, begining with the most fair-minded members of your various work groups. Validation from others makes you feel less isolated in your struggle to affect the power relations around you. (It is too easy to doubt your own perceptions when it appears everyone regards as unremarkable the very behavior that you regard as destructive to teamwork and creativity.)

Because our presence, particularly at the higher levels, breaks up the familiar all-boy routine, even the most courteous of men are still learning to stifle the urge to put the blame for everyone's social discomfort on us. But let's not lose hope. Today men perceptively (and ruefully) joke about about their own disruptive "testosterone displays" and are beginning to call one another on "whose is bigger" behavior.

In addition, recognition is growing for facilitative styles of sharing information, reducing tension in groups and working together in healthier ways. The trends toward self-managed work teams and concensus decision-making favor "influence" styles over "command and control" styles.

And finally, many men today are watching how we interact in business groups and want the energy that flows from the empowerment of every team member. They are noticing how women go about achieving it. Men increasingly appreciate the way women get on another person's wavelength and think *along with* someone else who is speaking. We encourage a speaker who is trying to tell us something by nodding and saying "uh-huh," by "hooking up." Our responses often include self-disclosure to build on what the speaker said and develop his or her themes. We generate information (and rapport) through attentive listening, asking questions, encouraging one another and volleying ideas rather than exercising topic control. Where many men dispute or ignore, most women connect, acknowledge and apply. "I'd like to tie in with what Sharon said earlier."

The usefulness of our communication strengths is validated by outside facilitators, team-building consultants and process observers who help shift work groups toward more productive interaction. Organization development consultants are trained to assist individuals and groups to substitute inclusive, egalitarian, team-focused approaches for win/lose habits.

While we're still stuck in the mud of this social transition, here are suggestions for a few specific situations.

Male colleagues often fail to register a woman's idea but if another man later offers the same suggestion they acknowledge it as brilliant and credit it to him. If a man seems to be running off with credit for an idea originally posed by a woman, point it out. "I don't think we could correctly term that 'Bill's resolution' since it is an elaboration of what Amy said an hour ago." Or, "Bill, I like your modification of Amy's suggestion." Don't let anyone hijack your contributions, either. Jump right in with "Oh, I'm glad you all have picked up on my suggestion. I was afraid at last week's meeting that you hadn't heard me."

A leader does not suffer unreasonable fear of reasonable risk. If stomach acid is already flowing like a river, why not confront what is really going on. If you can see that all the women have lowered their eyes, folded their arms and started to withdraw, say, "I'm beginning to get the feeling that several of us (a) disagree with what is going on, (b) feel Sharon's suggestion was dismissed too quickly, (c) are irritated.''

If you have to riffle through your papers or claw around inside your pocketbook or go to the restroom or speak to the person next to you, don't do it while another woman is talking. Congratulate, thank and praise one another on good points.

Notice how men and women take up space. Status hierarchies are often visible in the expansive relaxed obtrusive posture of the in-group and the constricted, circumspect, condensed posture of the out-group. Check yourself for defensive posture; rigidly clasped arms, for instance. Does your face feel pinched and drawn? If you modify your tight body language perhaps you will feel an uptick in your confidence and determination.

Sometimes we hate the inane rivalries and contests that go on in meetings so much that we feel we don't want to have to prove anything or argue for anything ever again. Perhaps the most powerful strategy for managing the stress is to speak frankly with other women about real problems, real issues and real feelings. Make it a point to do regular reality checking with other women.

## A Word About Panels

A panel is usually made up of three or more speakers and a moderator. The purpose is to provide the audience with several perspectives on a single topic. A panel can be made up of speakers who have different kinds of expertise in a general area; it is a good idea to enrich panels by keeping sex, race, age and other elements of diversity in mind, too. Panelists may agree or disagree with one another; all they need to have in common is the topic and coordination by a neutral moderator.

The moderator makes opening remarks and introduces each speaker. A good moderator will talk to all the panelists before the day of the presentation to elicit enough information to introduce each of them well and to be certain that they are all aware of what the others plan to say so there will be no duplication of speeches. She stipulates the time limit for their presentations, and informs them about the timing and format of the question-and-answer session.

A moderator does not deliver a presentation herself. It is her job to maintain a firm hand and benign air, to nag speakers who are talking too softly to be heard and to make sure each panelist observes her time limit by interrupting speakers who declaim beyond their fair share of the time.

The moderator makes transitional remarks between speakers. (For example, "Judge Myopia has refuted the idea that there are links between poverty and probable cause. Thank you, Judge. Ms. Monk, who has an opposing view, will tell us how poor people's rights are compromised in recordless lower courts. Ms. Monk?") After the last speaker has finished, the moderator opens the panel to questions from the audience. If there are no questions, the moderator asks one herself. The moderator prods, coaxes (and plants) good questions—she also tries to clarify (or paraphrase) ambiguous questions or answers. (In some cases, time is allotted for the speakers on the panel to question one another or respond to other speakers' statements.) It is the moderator's job to call on audience members and to direct their questions to panel members—this is to prevent one panelist from monopolizing the question-and-answer period. The moderator wraps up the session on a brief note of appreciation.

Panels are usually fun for speakers and audiences alike because of the variety of opinions and because there is time for informal exchange among panelists and audience. As a panelist you can think of it as a bridge game—you must play not only your own hand but also your partner's. It is a team speech, so you need to know what the others plan to talk about. A panel is a cooperative venture even when the speakers disagree, and it can be exhilarating to reason, discuss and differ together.

# CHAPTER TWELVE

## Media

### The Telephone

Effective communication does not mean making great speeches. It means great habits. Think of non-routine phone calls as a speech—that is, a form of self-presentation for which you have objectives, must organize your ideas and communicate them well. You have an audience for a phone call; you can connect with that audience well or poorly. Too often we pick up the phone impulsively and begin the dialogue before we have planned what we want to say or how we want to say it. Hence, we have conversations that drag on interminably in which we fail to persuade, do not get what we want and do not say what we meant to say. While few of us would make a too-hasty call to a prospective employer, many of us treat phone calls far less seriously than we would a face-to-face conversation or personal interview.

Consider, as you would in an impromptu speech, what you

want the point or conclusion of the conversation to be. Prepare opening "lines" to broach difficult topics. Make notes before calling so you won't have to phone back over and over with details you forgot to mention in the first call. We also suggest you make notes while you are conversing. If you jot down a point you want to respond to, you can return to active listening. It is difficult to concentrate on what someone is saying if you are simultaneously trying to hold your own point in mind for the next pause.

Begin conversations by clearing the time: "This isn't a good time for me to talk. May I return your call at three?" "I'd like to talk to you for about ten minutes. Is this a good time for you?" "I can only talk for a few minutes and then I have to write my column."

It may be an astonishingly useful and revealing exercise to tape record your side of a few phone conversations. Listen critically for voice quality, passive or aggressive approaches to discussion, vocalized pauses, and maddening recurrences of fillers such as "I mean," "like" or "y'know."

On the telephone, just as on radio, your warmth, sincerity and your mood must be expressed by your voice alone because the listener cannot see you. Body language, facial animation and physical appearance don't count. Attach stickers to your phones for visual reminders to keep your pitch low, your volume adequate and your "ums" to a minimum.

Before you dial, consider this: anytime an idea, a proposal or a request calls for a change in the current handling of affairs, it requires a personal oral presentation. Documents, letters, electronic mail and phone calls may precede or follow such a meeting, but they are not persuasive in themselves.

The message is simple: If you are serious about getting something you want, present it yourself, in person. On the phone, people tend to be impersonal. It is fairly easy to say "no" on the telephone. Saying no and being unreasonable face to face is something else again.

# Radio and TV

"Talk" has become a spectator sport. If you have success at anything from bank robbery to bird-watching, sooner or later you will be invited to converse for the benefit of an eavesdropping public. If you have never been in the studio audience for a talk show or witnessed a radio broadcast, we encourage you to do so as soon as it is practical. Once you've been inside a studio, seen the sets and learned how things work, you'll feel more prepared.

Most local television talk-show producers have trouble filling their studios with audiences day in and day out; sometimes station employees are dragged away from their desks to sit in for an hour to swell the crowd. Some stations have to award prizes or gifts to entice people. Find out which local programs welcome live audiences, when they tape and what time you have to arrive. College radio stations are often casual about studio visitors; it is better if you know someone who can escort you around, but even if you don't you will probably be able to sit in on a show.

Television stations offer air time to the community for Public Service Announcements. Call or write your local station to ask for information on PSA's. After you have read the rules, you will probably realize that several issues you care a lot about would be appropriate topics for PSA's. You may belong to some interest group that wants to communicate a message; a PSA is a good way to speak out. You can write and submit a PSA either as an individual or as an authorized representative of a group.

Station technicians realize that almost everyone who tapes a PSA is going on the air for the first time. They usually allow a few minutes for you to rehearse once or twice before taping. A Public Service Announcement taping is great practice in establishing eye contact with a camera and using a TelePrompTer.

If you are being considered for a guest appearance on a news broadcast or a talk show, a staff member (usually an assistant producer) will phone you to ask about your subject. Such a call is really an audition; if you don't come across well, an invitation might not be extended. If "Good Morning America" catches you in a bad moment, explain that you have Tom Cruise on the other line and ask when you can ring them back.

*When you are the guest.* Don't be surprised to discover that the cordial and sympathetic moderator who chats with you before you go on the air becomes the "role incumbent" as soon as the red lights flash. Her job is to get an exciting and entertaining interview. Just because the host meets you and "warms you up" doesn't mean that she will gently skirt subject areas you don't want to discuss, or will try to avoid upsetting you or will have the common decency not to ask embarrassing personal questions on the air. Producers and on-air talent are calm and friendly with guests before going on the air because a terrified guest is a stiff one. Once the tape is rolling, the gentle host may see her job as putting you on the spot. To her, your comfort will be secondary to a memorable interview.

"Off-the-record conversations?" Don't be naive. Requests to stay away from certain subjects will do absolutely no good if the show starts to drag. The host's priority is vitality, and she or he will sensationalize a segment if necessary.

The best way to avoid trouble in a radio or television interview is to give them the electricity they want in the first place. Present your interviewer-to-be and the show's producer with a suggestion list of hard-hitting questions before air time. You don't have to be at cross-purposes with them; a lively conversation also serves your best interests. Prepare answers that supply drama or controversy so the host won't have to go poking for it.

Also send the producer basic information about your topic.

Make the info sheets concise; most talk show hosts don't read an author's book, for instance, before (or after) interviewing the author. Radio and television programming is aimed to appeal to the "broadest" possible market. That means producers not only assume total ignorance on the part of listeners and viewers, they contribute to it.

Be prepared to give basic definitions of your terms and a general explanation of your topic because the producer's premise is that the audience has zero information. Remember, too, that anecdotes and examples work better than abstract explanations; they are more fun.

*Don't fear repeating yourself.* An actor is used to getting up in front of an audience night after night and saying the same lines with all the emotion she can. The rest of us feel inauthentic repeating ourselves. We want to appear unstudied, unrehearsed and natural. Most of us are self-conscious and embarrassed repeating a story in front of someone who has already heard us tell it. Instead of repeating the story the best way, we change it so it will seem original or spontaneous to listeners who have heard it before. The host, producer and other station employees who talk to you before the show want to hear what you plan to say on the air. Later, you must forget they've heard it. Say what you came to say uninhibited by the fact that you are repeating yourself.

Programs are usually edited only if the guest says something obscene or slanderous. Your show will be aired with whatever mistakes, pauses or fumblings you commit. The only difference between a taped show and a live show is the broadcast date.

## Radio

No one can see you. You don't have to worry about eye contact or appearing nervous. Your movements don't have to be controlled and your hair doesn't have to be combed.

Yet, like any other speech situation, preparation and "spontaneity" are mutually reinforcing, not mutually exclusive. Bring an outline with you so you are sure to get in what you want to say.

*Do your homework.* Find out ahead of time exactly what is going to happen. How long will the interview last? Will there be phone calls, music breaks or commercials to interrupt your interview?

If the show is a call-in, plant a lot of calls and questions with relatives and friends. Ask them to write the station after the show to thank the producers for bringing such a fascinating topic and guest to the air, and to request more programs on your topic.

*At the studio.* An engineer will do a sound check before you tape/go on the air. If you pop your *p*'s or hiss your *s*'s, you may be asked to speak across your mike rather than directly into it. This means that the mike will be turned, or that your chair will be placed at a new angle. When it is time for the voice check, turn to the moderator and begin an animated lowdown on your name and address and the subjects for tonight's show just as though you are on the air. It drives engineers up the parapets when a guest can't think of anything to say for the voice check, or recites the alphabet in a mousy, hesitant way then proceeds to use an entirely different volume level when she actually speaks on the air. When you are miked for a speech before an audience you stand back far enough (and/or have the sound level adjusted) so that you still have to project your voice. In radio, too, the ideal is to speak in normal tones, not soft ones. Low volume communicates low energy.

Many radio producers ask guests to wear headsets, especially if there are several guests on the air at the same time. Headphones are a bit uncomfortable, and make you look funny, but they let you hear what the audience hears. You can tell instantly when you are not speaking directly into the mike, making too

*Standby:* A warning signal to tell the engineer that you want her to be ready to do something.

*Start it or do it:* Tells the engineer to do whatever it is she is supposed to do next. Usually it means to start a tape. You should spell out what you expect in advance.

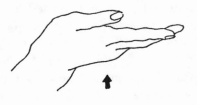

*Fade-up:* Increase the volume level of whatever's on the air. In the case of a "voice-over" this means increase the music level.

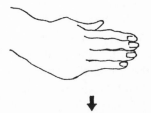

*Fade down:* Decrease the level of whatever's on the air.

*Microphone on the air:* This tells the engineer to put your mike on.

*Cut the mike:* Takes you off the air.

*Station break:* A pause in the program to give the station I.D. which consists of the call letters and the city in which the station is located. I.D.'s should be given as close to the hour as possible, every hour, at a natural break in the program.

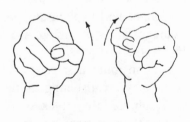

*Roll theme:* Tells the engineer to start your theme music. In cases when you are "backtiming" your show to end at the logged time exactly, the theme should be started, but not faded up until the rest of the program has ended.

much racket flipping through your notes or tapping your teeth with your pencil. If you hear yourself sounding weak and far-away, it is probably because you have turned your head to one side to look at the guest sitting next to you. Eye contact stimu-lates energy, because the response from another person turns us on; yet if you go "off mike," all is lost.

*During the program.* Heed the warnings station employees give you about their equipment. If their equipment is old and unsophisticated, you won't be able to move around much with-out going out of microphone range. If you bump or tap the mike it will probably broadcast thunderously.

Lean forward in your chair to feel (and therefore sound) more animated. Do not pick up the mike or move it. Don't wear clanky jewelry and, finally, don't drink a carbonated beverage before or during the show.

The host and the engineer will use hand signals to communi-cate with each other when you are on the air. (We have included a chart of a few common moderator's signals for you.) The moderator will explain any gestures that are meant for you (for example, a "wrap it up, we're running out of time" signal). Ignore the rest.

Bear in mind that people can't absorb as much information when they are listening as they can when they are reading. If your subject is complex or if you use numbers it is very im-portant to paraphrase, to give clear examples and to repeat. Also repeat key ideas. Remember some of your listeners just jumped into the car and turned on the radio. Write the name of the host and anyone else on the air with you on a cue card so you won't forget their names during the conversation.

Radio flattens a speaker out. If you are a slow speaker, put "speed up" reminders in front of you. (Fast talkers sound better on the radio than they do in real life.) An audience that can see you will wait patiently while you fumble for a word or think of a response to a question. On the radio this is called "dead air" and it is what every announcer dreads. Listeners who are fiddling with the dial pass right over a silent station.

A good radio announcer (and guest) presents everything as though it just occurred to her for the first time at that very moment. The excitement in an amateur's voice depends in part on how involved she can be with the person with whom she is talking. Well, good luck. Much of the time the host will be focused on other tasks, and looking away from you to signal the engineer, consulting her notes while you talk, watching the buttons on her phone setup and so on. It isn't easy to converse like this, but just keep rolling as though you had her undivided attention. Rivet your face to hers for those moments when she *is* able to reestablish real contact. Talk to your lap and your voice will die.

*Call-in shows.* Almost all of the calls you receive will be from individuals who want to disagree with your point of view and/or who tuned in late, misunderstood your point of view and want to disagree or ask irrelevant questions. The people who are motivated to call are usually the ones who are angry with you. This is a built-in fact of radio life rather than a reflection of how well you've articulated your position. Be gracious. Don't get upset or sidetracked. Stick to the points.

When you allow yourself to sound exasperated or arrogant, you are forgetting that the caller's views represent the views of thousands of others—and that you're turning off the un-committed. It is the show host's job to cut people off, not yours.

Be brief if calls are coming in thick and fast. If the switch-board isn't lighting up, keep talking. Your list of subsidiary points and issues will help. Remember that this radio conversa-tion is just like any other speech—if you aren't getting the response you want, your natural tendency may be to get safer, smaller and duller, to pretend you aren't there or that you don't care. Go to the other extreme, behave as though everything were just fine. And remember, the worst thing that can happen on radio is dead air.

## Television

> "If I could I would always work in silence and obscurity, and let my efforts be known by their results."
>
> —Emily Brontë

*Before the television show.* Try on your clothes *seated* in front of a mirror. Avoid white, vivid patterns, small busy prints, flashy jewelry that may catch the lights, anything that makes noise when you move, necklines you must clutch or hemlines you must tug. Don't wear slacks that ride halfway up your calf when you're seated. If you wear a dress or a skirt, pay special attention to length. Do you want your hemline down over your thighs on the air? We hope so, but that's us.

Television lights are hot. Aren't you glad we reminded you about dress shields? Take a jacket or sweater to the studio (where the air conditioning gives new meaning to the phrase "flash frozen") to wear just until you step up on the set, where the lights will be uncomfortably warm.

Watch the show a few times before your appearance on it to see what kind of posture seems to work best for guests who occupy the chair you will soon occupy.

Do not touch the equipment. A microphone will be fastened to your clothes by a union member, who will probably be male.

*On the air.* Enjoy the attention, because it will be over in a hurry. As a guest on a talk show you can be conversational, informal and colloquial. Unless you *want* to appear furtive, keep your eye contact with the interviewer steady and sustained. This is one time you do *not* aspire to make eye contact with everyone in the room. If you look out into the studio audience, or at the technicans and camera crew to try to include them in what you are saying, the impression on the viewers at home will be that your eyes are wandering all over the place. The viewers cannot see who it is you are trying to include.

The exception is when a statement you are making is being filmed or videotaped. In this case, look directly into the camera, just as though the camera were another person in the audience. The result is that the audience viewing the film later will feel included.

The camera with the red light on is the one in use. There are two, three or sometimes more cameras rolling around; the one in use will keep changing. Ignore them. Just talk to the host.

Keep your hands away from your face and avoid jerky movements. Don't whip your head around from host to fellow guest and back. Leisurely movements are best, such as when you change position in your chair. If you are given a swivel chair, do not swivel.

Television combines long shots with close-ups. The movement of the eyelid or eyebrow, or the quiver of the lips that might be perfectly eloquent will be lost on a long shot, while an expressive movement of the arm will be lost in a close-up where only the facial movements can be seen. The only solution is to be yourself and hope the odds are with you; some of your facial animation will be captured and so will some of your deadpan or severe expressions.

Television will make you appear about ten pounds heavier. And anybody who sits in the director's booth, or operates the lights or cameras who wants to make you look absolutely terrible can do it. It is small comfort, we know, but it isn't always our fault when we appear lumbering, slow and undereducated.

In a "direct" interview you will be instructed to address the camera. It's artificial and awkward, but keep your eyes glued to that camera fulltime! Otherwise, ignore the camera. Politicians (on shows like "Meet the Press," for example) often turn away from the questioner and speak straight into the camera. The jury's still out; some viewers experience this as aggressive, too much of a hard sell.

Your attitude toward the host is crucial. If you want the audience to care about you, you have to show that you care about them. You do that through the person of the interviewer. You express how happy you are to be with the audience by a warm attitude toward the host. Treat the interviewer as if he or she is a welcome guest in *your* home. In other words, mentally take on the role of host. The moderator may not stifle his impatience, boredom or anger (except when he or she is on camera), but always stifle yours. If you are challenged with a hostile or rude question answer with humor, or at least politely. At that moment, what you say will count far less than the way you say it.

Technicians, camera operators and other staff members frequently talk and laugh off camera. Block them out. Focus on the interviewer. Mention your product/book/company a few times but don't overdo it. The producer of the show is trying to sustain the illusion that your appearance is news or entertainment, not a commercial.

*What's your headline?* Inexperienced "guests" make three primary errors. First, they assume reporters have done their homework so they sit back and wait for the right questions to be asked. Second, they feel compelled to answer any question regardless of how irrelevant, antagonistic or just plain stupid it might be. Third, they lack a message.

Ask the producer how long your segment/interview will run. Most interviews are very short—about four minutes—and what the audience hears first will make the sharpest impression. Write out a focused and vivid eighty-word statement. Memorize it. Write out a second, somewhat shorter statement, which makes the same point in different words. Your goal is to work in both statements during the interview. Anecdotes, even in a short interview, catch attention.

You are as much in charge of the interview as the host, and you probably have more at stake. Feel free to steer the conversation with such expressions as "incidentally," "in addition to that," "even more amazing" and so on.

## Meet the Press

> "I don't care what you write as long as you spell my name right."
> —American cliché

The saying "I don't care what they say about me as long as they're talking about me" had better have some validity for your situation before you take your case to the public. The chances of accurate reporting of your views, issue or event are slim, so the first consideration is whether it's worth the risk to get media attention at all. By all means, tape your remarks in a press interview or at a press conference and certainly have copies of the text of any statement you make. But don't count on a correction, a retraction or an apology if you are misquoted.

Reporters are people. Each reporter brings to a news event limited information, exposure, intelligence, analytical ability and time. Each reporter has different ideas about what is newsworthy. Each reporter has an interest in writing "good" copy, and sometimes that interest conflicts with what she perceives as the dull news you have to offer. Each reporter has limitations of space, and often oversimplifies or omits the context for facts or statements you provide. This may mean that your news is distorted or falsified. The jackal journalism emphasis on celebrity, gossip and sleaze is stronger than ever while "hard" news budgets are suffering.

Readers are no more discriminating than reporters; it is amazing how often an article that you perceive as "damaging" to you turns out not to be. Ask which risk is greater: to have readers know something incorrect or to know nothing at all.

If you are a participant in a press conference, you and the other speakers will each deliver a brief prepared statement. Rehearse your statement thoroughly so that you can say it to the camera/audience, only checking with your notes from time to time. By all means, look alive while the others are talking. It would be just your luck to have your finger in your nose when the crew is collecting cutaways (reaction shots and color shots).

News producers often decide what to broadcast on the basis of what they have the footage to support, not on the basis of what is most important for the audience to know. This is a "photo op," not just a "word op." Plan movement (such as presenting, signing, demonstrating or displaying something). You are more likely to appear on television or be photographed if your news involves something visual. It helps if the setting for the press conference is visually interesting. Pay attention to the background/backdrop. Seat the speakers close enough together so that the television crews will have no trouble filming everyone from the same spot.

The television crew and press photographers may ask you to repeat your statement or the presentation of the award several times or go on endlessly shaking hands and grinning until they have it on tape the way they want it.

You have very little time in a press conference. Reporters are always in a hurry. Begin on time and don't waste time answering irrelevant questions. Expect antagonism. In our era of sensationalism, reporters want you to make colorful statements and may try to get you riled up to get them. Don't allow anyone or anything to take you off your points. "That is an interesting point/question, but even more fascinating is . . ."; "I'll be glad to answer that for you later. Right now I think most people are wondering. . . ." Irrelevant questions absorb precious minutes you need to deliver your message. Yes, be quotable, but not on extraneous matters.

It helps to be cordial to reporters. Feature writers get to say what kind of impression you made and pass along value judgments on you. If you are charming, warm and funny they may say so. If you are cranky they'll say that, too. But acting gracious and devoting all the time the reporter requests to provide background information will not guarantee accuracy. Reporters are interested in what sells papers. Complex and difficult analysis does not sell papers. Media will print/air what is accessible. Yes, try to provide the background, the context, the facts that make what you say comprehensible. Yes, be courteous and yes, dodge irrelevant questions. But give short answers when you can and expect out-of-context quotes when you can't. Use examples to support your generalizations. And finally, don't become so excited you say something you want to take back later. Whenever you are interviewed at a press conference or for an on-the spot news item, do your best to keep your pitch down, speak deliberately and avoid wild exaggeration. ("The filthy capitalist supermarket owners will be brought to their knees by our boycott. We won't stand for it and neither of us is afraid to say so!") Bear in mind that your statements may sound completely hysterical in contrast to the custard-smooth reporters.

# CHAPTER THIRTEEN

# Final Thoughts

> *"If you want to hit the jackpot,
> you have to put a coin in the
> machine."*
> —Flip Wilson

*Just do it.* If, after having carefully read and taken to heart every word in this book, you still feel inadequate, inarticulate and unequal to the task, here's our advice: do it anyway. Hardly anybody feels completely comfortable speaking in public. Nobody can handle herself with sureness and grace every time. At some point one simply has to throw oneself into the lake and hope to swim. You don't have to be wonderful to have a right to be heard. You just have to close your eyes and jump.

We would a thousand times rather see women standing up boring everyone to death, going blank, screeching, giggling and making no sense at all than sitting in the back of the room keeping their mouths shut because they are too intimidated to take the risk. We've all done that and know it is a dead end. Speaking up is better.

*And do it your way.* Homogenization is for dairies; integrate but don't assimilate. The dominant try to keep themselves domi-

210

nant by enforcing their standards about How Things Are Done. The unspoken message from the beginning has been "If you want to play on our turf, the least you can do is play by our rules." You don't need to mimic any particular style or adopt anybody else's ineffective behavior.

Do people at your meetings brief the group without notes (and ramble, forget key points, render simple concepts incoherent?). Break the mold! Use notes.

Do members of your committee remain seated when they talk (never mind that only their near neighbors can see or hear them properly?). Break the mold! Rise to speak.

Do some men in your division unconsciously exclude women from the handshake culture? Include yourself by forcefully extending your hand. Does everyone at your staff meeting get the same amount of time to speak, but with your accent, nobody can understand you if you speak that quickly? Insist on accommodation. When your group is teleconferencing, is your dark-skinned face a blur on the television screen because the lighting is set for the white folks? Hey! Speak up!

> "Cautious, careful people always casting about to preserve their reputation or social standards can never bring about a reform."
> —Susan B. Antony

Do the other members of your section listen to managment's pious bombast with ingratiating little smiles? The road to hell is paved with such silences. Break the mold. Ask the taboo questions. Confront the tough issues with integrity *and* compassion. Be grateful when others also challenge you. We suffer recurring environmental, economic and racial nightmares not because some spoke too well, but because others spoke not at all ... waiting for the perfect moment, waiting for the perfect words, waiting for a time when more standing in the organization will provide safe cover and add clout. We urge you to contribute your perspective, bring heretical ideas to the table and refuse to be bought.

"To a worm in horseradish the
whole world is horseradish."
—Old Yiddish saying

## Resisting Assimilation

We teach public speaking workshops for women employed by our client organizations because we understand that there is a profound link between speech and power. We have been moved and inspired by the legion of our students who have translated their caring from hand-wringing to action.

As we advance in our careers, at every stage we may be the newest, most tentatively accepted, most marginal members of our organizations. Despite this, many women have risked everything to blow the whistle, to call things by their right names, to avoid the "go along/get along" bureaucratic mentality. Instead of allowing themselves to be re-socialized, such women have begun the process of reforming and transforming "business as usual." Many have had to invent themselves. Like millions of other ordinary women, our workshop graduates have spoken up in the teeth of relentless pressure to conform (compounded by fear of economic penalties). It has been a privilege to work with you.

We hope our book will help you, too, to find your backbone, cling to your values and speak up.

*"We must take our little teaspoons and get to work.*
*We can't wait for the shovels."*
—Florynce Kennedy

# NOTES

## Chapter Two

1 Marjorie Swacker; Myra and David Sadker ("Sexism in the Schoolroom of the '80s"; Dale Spender *(Man Made Language)*, Carole Edelsky ("Who's Got the Floor?").

2 Barbara and Gene Eakins.

3 Candace West and Don Zimmerman, 1983. "Small Insults: A Study of Interruptions in Cross-Sex Conversations Between Unacquainted Persons"; 1985; Eakins and Eakins; Greif.

4 Robin Lakoff, *Language and Woman's Place,* p. 4.

5 Jacqueline Sachs.

6 Patricia Hayes Bradley.

## Chapter Five

7 The ideas for this example were taken from Del Martin, *Battered Wives*.

## Chapter Six

8 Barbara Garson, *All the Livelong Day.*

**Chapter Nine**

9 Robin Lakoff, *Language and Woman's Place,* p. 40.

**Chapter Eleven**

10 Myra and David Sadker, "Sexism in the Schoolroom of the '80s."

11 Dale Spender, *Man Made Language;* Carole Edelsky, "Who's Got the Floor?"

# BIBLIOGRAPHY

Bartlett, John: *Familiar Quotations,* 16th edition, Justin Kaplan, Editor, Little, Brown and Company, Boston, 1992.

Doyle, Michael and David Straus: *How to Make Meetings Work: The New Interaction Method;* Wyden Books, 1985.

Faludi, Susan: *Backlash: The Undeclared War Against American Women,* Crown, New York, 1991.

Fillmore, Mary: *Women MBA's: A Foot in the Door,* G. K. Hall, Boston, 1987. Although directed particularly at women considering the degree, each chapter is loaded with practical advice about handling workplace realities all of us face.

Fisher, Roger and William Ury: *Getting to Yes: Negotiating Agreement Without Giving In,* Penguin Books, New York, 1985.

Flexner, Eleanor: *Century of Struggle: The Woman's Rights Movement in the United States,* Atheneum, New York, 1968. Basic history of the first wave of feminism in the United States.

Follett, Wilson: *Modern American Usage.* Warner Books, New York, 1974.

Garson, Barbara: *All the Livelong Day: The Meaning and De-meaning of Routine Work,* Doubleday and Company, Inc., New York, 1975.

Henley, Nancy: *Body Politics,* Prentice-Hall, New Jersey, 1977. Highly recommended. Excellent reading about power, sex and nonverbal communication.

Lakoff, Robin: *Language and Woman's Place,* Harper Colophon Books, New York, 1975.

Lash, Joseph P.: *Eleanor and Franklin,* Signet, New York, 1973. Includes how Eleanor Roosevelt learned to speak in public.

Miller, Casey, and Kate Swift: *Words and Women,* Doubleday (Anchor Press), New York, 1976. Why *Modern American Usage* is often wrong even though "correct."

Robert, Henry: *Robert's Rules of Order*, William Morrow, New York, 1971.

Roget, Peter Mark: *New Roget's Thesaurus in Dictionary Form,* G. P. Putnam's Sons, New York, 1978.

Sarnoff, Dorothy: *Speech Can Change Your Life,* Dell Publishing Company, Inc., New York, 1972.

Strunk, William, and E. B. White: *Elements of Style,* Macmillan, New York, 1972.

Tannen, Deborah: *You Just Don't Understand,* Ballantine Books, New York, 1990.

Wolf, Naomi: *The Beauty Myth,* Bantam, New York, 1992.

# ABOUT THE AUTHORS

Speaking Up<sup>SM</sup> is a small woman-owned national consulting firm that has offered public speaking and career development training to women since 1974. Our clients are corporations and federal agencies. For information about speeches, workshops or ordering books in bulk, write to:

**Speaking Up**
**1750 Vallejo Street, Suite 301**
**San Francisco, CA 94123-5028**

Janet Stone considers that only the dead are neutral. A career of advocacy always struck her as more lively than a career of neutrality. She is coauthoring a how-to book with Mary Fillmore for support services staffers who want to move up or into another field.

Jane Bachner has had poems published by *Centennial Review, Connecticut River Review, Earth's Daughters, Rhino, Birmingham Poetry Review, Poetpourri, Lip Service, Paintbrush,*

*Kennesaw Review, Negative Capability, The Magee Park Anthology,* and *San Diego Writers' Monthly.* She won first prize in the 1988 Johanna B. Bourgoyne poetry contest sponsored by *Amelia* magazine and honorable mention in the 1991 Awards Edition of *Poetpourri.* She has just completed a book of short stories called *Living in California.*